Cubase® SX 3 Ignite!

Eric Grebler

Chris Hawkins

THOMSON

COURSE TECHNOLOGY

Professional ■ Trade ■ Reference

Cubase® SX 3 Ignite!

SVP, Thomson Course Technology PTR: Andy Shafran; Publisher: Stacy L. Hiquet; Senior Marketing Manager: Sarah O'Donnell; Marketing Manager: Heather Hurley; Manager of Editorial Services: Heather Talbot; Senior Acquisitions Editor: Todd Jensen; Senior Editor: Mark Garvey; Associate Marketing Manager: Kristin Eisenzopf; Marketing Coordinator: Jordan Casey; Project Editor: Jenny Davidson; Technical Reviewer: Greg Ondo; PTR Editorial Services Coordinator: Elizabeth Furbish; Interior Layout Tech: Marian Hartsough; Cover Designer: Mike Tanamachi; Indexer: Sharon Shock; Proofreader: Sara Gullion

ISBN: 1-59200-538-1

Library of Congress Catalog Card Number: 2004114496

Printed in the United States of America

04 05 06 07 08 BH 10 9 8 7 6 5 4 3 2 1

THOMSON

COURSE TECHNOLOGY

Professional ■ Trade ■ Reference

Thomson Course Technology PTR,
a division of Thomson Course Technology
25 Thomson Place
Boston, MA 02210
http://www.courseptr.com

Acknowledgments

I would like to acknowledge the efforts of all the people at Course Technology PTR who made this project possible. In particular I would like to point out the efforts of Jenny Davidson, who acted as chief cook and bottle washer on this project. Thanks must also be extended to Chris Hawkins who provided the foundation for most of this book. I'd like to also thank my wife Kara, my son Ethan, and the rest of my friends and family for their support and encouragement.

About the Author

ERIC GREBLER is an IT professional, author, and certified trainer who has demystified the world of computers for thousands of people. Eric has written books, developed curriculum, and created material on a wide range of technical topics, including desktop publishing, digital audio sequencing, graphics, XML, and operating systems.

When he's not writing books, he can be found changing diapers, mixing formula, and singing nursery rhymes.

Contents at a Glance

Contents

Introduction

This *Ignite!* series book will help you understand, use, and explore the world of Cubase SX 3. This digital music production software provides you with a variety of approaches to create, edit, manage, and distribute your musical projects. In this latest version, many changes have been made to simplify the user experience and increase the functionality of different tools.

This book provides you with a visual reference to learn the components of Cubase SX 3. Each step-by-step instruction is accompanied by a screen capture showing you exactly where to click to accomplish a task. It clearly illustrates how to complete common tasks and provides you with tips and shortcuts along the way. You won't be inundated with a lot of technology terms and complicated descriptions. This book cuts through the fat and takes you straight to the meat of learning the software.

Who Should Read This Book

If you are ready to explore the world of music sequencing on the desktop, then this book is for you. This book is designed as a self-paced guide for users who are new to Cubase SX. It will give you a solid foundation so that you can progress to the next level of knowledge. Obviously, no book can teach you everything there is to know about one topic. The goal of this book is to give you an introduction to Cubase and teach you how to use many of the different tools that it has to offer.

How the Book Works

There are a variety of exercises in this book that you can follow by using tutorials that can be downloaded through the Course Technology PTR website. Don't worry if you do not have access to the Internet; you can still follow these tutorials by using your own files. The tutorials themselves can be found at **www.courseptr.com/downloads**.

Throughout the book, I included tips and cautions. Here are examples of what you'll see:

TIP

Tips help you find faster shortcuts such as key commands that will help you improve your workflow when using Cubase SX 3.

CAUTION

Cautions help you avoid traps or pitfalls.

NOTE

Notes provide you with additional information.

1

Setting Up SX for Your Computer

Welcome to the wonderful world of Cubase, the leading application for composing, recording, and producing music. The tools available to you in Cubase are of a professional level; with help from this book, in no time you will be using these tools to create professional-sounding music of your own. Assuming that you have already installed Cubase, we are ready to dive in. We'll begin by making a few adjustments to Cubase's settings in order to optimize its performance.

In this chapter, you'll learn how to:

- Launch Cubase SX
- Optimize your audio hardware
- Optimize your MIDI hardware

Starting Cubase

To access all of Cubase's great features and tools, you'll need to launch the program.

Starting Cubase for Windows Users

Windows users can launch the application by using the Start menu.

1. Click on the **Start menu**. The Start menu will appear.

2. Click on **All Programs**. The Programs menu will appear.

3. Click on the **Steinberg Cubase SX 3 menu**. The Cubase menu will appear.

4. Click on **Cubase SX3**. The Cubase splash screen will appear followed by the application itself.

NOTE

Starting Cubase for Macintosh Users

Macintosh users can find the Cubase SX application in the Applications folder. If you click on the Go menu, then click Applications, the Applications Finder window will appear. You can then locate and double-click on the Cubase SX icon and the application will launch.

TIP

Launching from the Dock

Copying the Application icon to the dock will allow you to quickly access the program without having to open the Applications folder.

Audio Card Setup— VST Multitrack

By default, Cubase is set up to run with very few problems on a typical machine. However, in most cases a modern machine will be able to outperform these "typical" settings. One of the areas that can be effectively tweaked is the audio card settings. Let's see how you can get the best possible performance from your audio card.

Latency—What Is It?

The point of tweaking your audio card is to improve its latency. *Latency* can be best described as a delay created by the fact that audio has to pass through your inputs, through Cubase, and then back to the card's outputs. Latency makes it difficult to monitor your playing as you add parts to your song. And latency also affects VST instruments—the delay will be apparent as you play the instrument from your MIDI controller (more on VST instruments in Chapter 8). Decreasing latency can take a toll on your computer's performance, though. Let's look at some ways to improve your system's latency.

How Can I Reduce Latency?

As you follow the next exercises, keep in mind that lowering the latency puts strain on your computer. Try to find a happy medium in which both the latency and the CPU usage are well balanced.

Windows XP—Using ASIO

In order for Cubase to pass information to the audio card, it must first travel through an "audio subsystem." This subsystem is primarily responsible for your system's latency. Computers running Windows can use one of two systems: the audio subsystem of the Windows operating system or the ASIO system. ASIO was developed by Steinberg to achieve better latencies within Cubase than the Windows system. In order for

ASIO to be fully optimized, an audio card requires a special ASIO driver. The good news is that many card manufacturers are now writing ASIO drivers. Check your audio card's documentation for ASIO support.

Now let's optimize your card.

1. **Click** on the **Devices menu**. The Devices menu will appear.

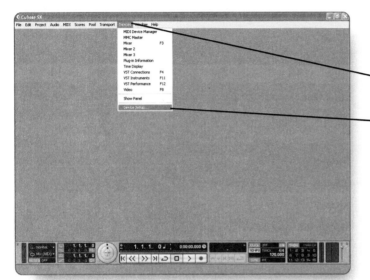

2. **Click** on **Device Setup**. The Device Setup window will appear. The left side of the window displays all the devices in use by Cubase; the right side displays the configuration settings for the currently selected device.

3. **Click** on **VST AudioBay**. The configurations of your audio card will appear. Cubase refers to these settings as the VST AudioBay settings.

Next we want to select the best possible driver.

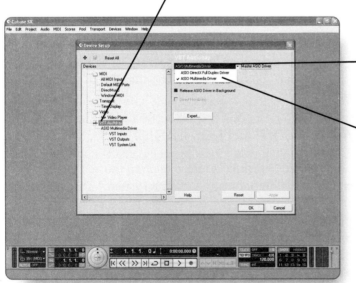

4. **Click** on the **ASIO Driver menu**. The list of available drivers will appear.

● **ASIO Multimedia driver**. This driver will use the audio subsystem of Windows XP. Latency is high with this driver.

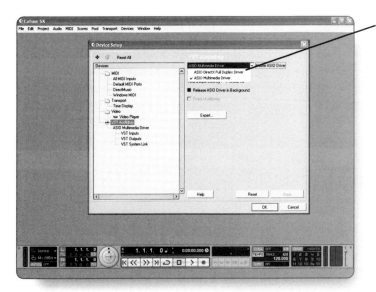

- **ASIO DirectX Full Duplex driver**. This driver uses the DirectSound audio subsystem of Windows; DirectSound is an extension of DirectX. This driver will provide better latencies than the ASIO Multimedia driver.

- **ASIO Specific driver**. If your audio card supports ASIO, the ASIO driver for your card will appear in the driver list. This driver (if available) provides the lowest possible latency.

- The latency, in measurements of milliseconds, is displayed under the ASIO Driver menu.

5. If you are using a card that comes with a specific ASIO driver (and it appears in the Driver menu), select this driver for optimum performance. If your card does not have ASIO drivers, your best option would be to use the DirectX Full Duplex driver. This driver will give you better latency than the Multimedia driver.

NOTE

Reducing Latency

If your card supports ASIO, you can further reduce the latency by making adjustments to the driver's control panel. Consult your card's documentation to learn about making control panel adjustments.

TIP

ASIO Audio Cards

If your audio card does not support ASIO, it may be a good idea to consider a card that does. Many cards now support this popular system, and they are becoming more affordable all the time.

Macintosh OS X—Core Audio

With Apple's OS X operating system, there is only one audio subsystem that can be used with SX: Core Audio, which was designed specifically for Apple's OS X. Card manufacturers do not have to write any additional special drivers for Core Audio; any card that works in OS X will work in Cubase SX.

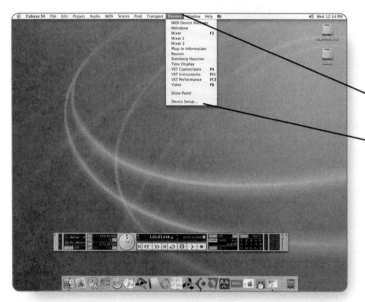

To set up SX with your audio card:

1. **Click** on the **Devices menu**. The Devices menu will appear.

2. **Click** on **Device Setup**. The Device Setup window will appear. The left side of the window displays all the connected devices; the right side displays the configuration settings for that device.

3. **Click** on **VST Multitrack**. The configurations of your audio card will appear. Cubase refers to the settings of your card as the VST Multitrack settings.

4. **Click** on the **ASIO Driver menu**. The list of installed cards with Core Audio drivers will appear.

5. **Click** on the **driver** of the audio card you want to use with SX.

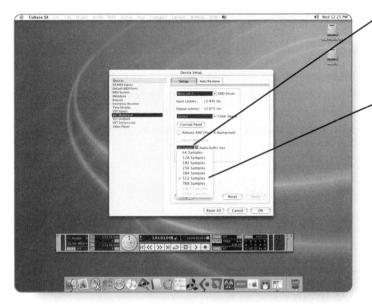

6. Click on the **Audio Buffer Size**. The audio card's available buffer sizes will appear in a drop-down menu.

7. Choose 512 from the menu. The Audio Buffer Size will affect the latency of your card. The lower the buffer size, the lower the latency; however, remember that the lower the latency, the harder your computer will need to work. 512 is typically a safe level, which will give you a latency of around 13 ms.

NOTE

Core Audio Drivers

In Mac OS X, SX also refers to the audio card drivers as ASIO drivers (Steinberg's audio subsystem for the Windows platform); however, the driver is in fact a Core Audio driver and not an ASIO driver.

MIDI Settings

Next we will make the necessary configuration changes to your MIDI hardware.

DirectMusic (Windows XP)—Core MIDI System (OS X)

DirectMusic is an extension of DirectX, and DirectX is an extension of the Windows XP operating system that provides enhancements for multimedia content. Cubase SX and SL use this system to provide the best possible performance for MIDI devices. For Macintosh OS X users, Cubase will use the Core MIDI System of OS X to provide optimal performance with MIDI devices. With the DirectMusic and MIDI System configuration page, you can choose which MIDI interfaces you want to use; you can also rename the MIDI interfaces, which can make it easier for you to keep track of them.

Activating and Deactivating MIDI Interfaces

Depending on your machine, you might have more than one MIDI interface, and may want to use only one of them. Using the DirectMusic (Windows) and MIDI System (Macintosh) configuration windows, you can tell SX which interfaces you want to use by enabling and disabling the installed interfaces.

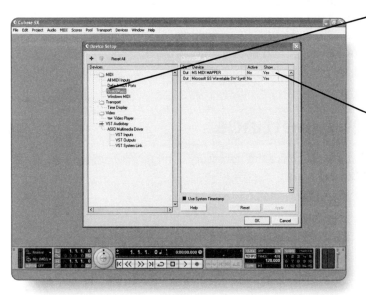

1. **Click** on **DirectMusic** (MIDI System for Macintosh OS X) from the Devices list. The DirectMusic/MIDI System configuration page will appear.

2. **Click** on **Yes** next to the interface that you want to disable under the Show column; the column will now read "No." The interface will no longer be available for use in Cubase.

NOTE

Reactivating the Interface

Simply repeat the preceding steps to reactivate the interface.

Renaming MIDI Interfaces

Cubase will get the name of all your MIDI interfaces from the driver that runs them. In some situations, the name may be long and confusing. You can rename the interfaces so that they are more manageable.

To rename the interfaces:

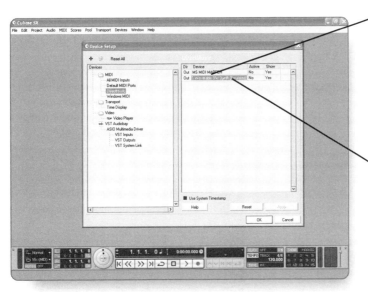

1. Click on the **MIDI interface's name** under the Device column. The name will become highlighted.

2. Type in the desired **name** for the interface and **press return**. The interface will be renamed.

• The Active column shows you if the interface is being used in a currently loaded project.

All MIDI Inputs

With the All MIDI Inputs page, you can determine which MIDI interfaces can be assigned to the MIDI input of a MIDI track (more on assigning inputs and outputs to MIDI tracks in Chapter 4).

To enable or disable a MIDI interface's input:

1. Click on **All MIDI Inputs** from the Devices list. The MIDI Inputs Configurations menu will appear.

2. Click on the **Active column** next to the MIDI interface you want to activate or deactivate.

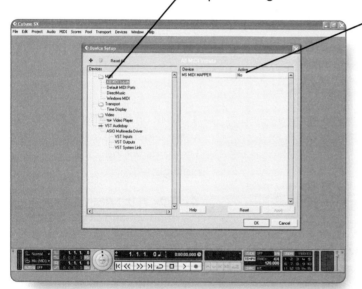

Default MIDI Ports

When you create a MIDI track, the inputs and outputs of that track will default to whatever interface is set in the Default MIDI Ports configuration. You might want to customize the default ports if you have several MIDI interfaces and a MIDI controller keyboard connected to one of them. You would most likely want it so that all new MIDI tracks automatically will be connected to the controller.

1. Click on **Default MIDI Ports** from the Devices list. The Default Ports configuration page will appear.

2. Click on the **MIDI Input menu** and choose the desired interface to be the default input.

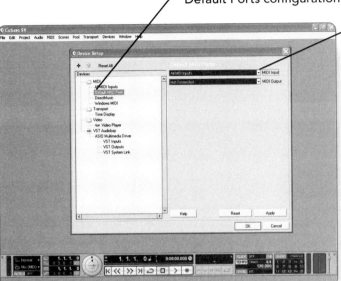

3. Click on the **MIDI Output menu** and choose the desired interface to be used as the default output.

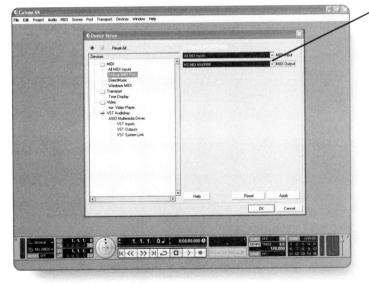

NOTE

Choosing MIDI Inputs

You also have the option to choose All MIDI Inputs as the default MIDI input; if you choose this, by default a MIDI track's input will be connected to all MIDI interfaces.

2

Creating a New Project–Project Templates

With all your hardware set up and ready to go, we are going to move on to creating your own project. We'll also take a look at how to use SX's templates to create customized projects that will improve your workflow.

In this chapter, you'll learn how to:

- Start new projects and adjust project settings
- Create and work with template files

Creating a New Project and Adjusting Settings

When working in Cubase SX everything you record, edit, or mix is stored in a project file. This project file holds all the relevant information pertaining to the project you are working on, such as the sound quality, the project length, as well as all recording, mixing, and editing information. Before you can begin to work in SX, you will need to create a new project.

NOTE

Songs or Projects?

Even though many users refer to projects as "songs," for the sake of consistency, throughout this book I'll refer to them as "projects." Project is more appropriate, since some users are using SX for non-musical work.

Creating a Blank Project

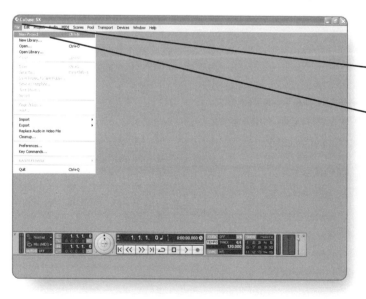

We'll begin by creating a blank project.

1. **Click** on the **File menu**. The File menu will appear.

2. **Click** on **New Project**. The New Project dialog window will appear.

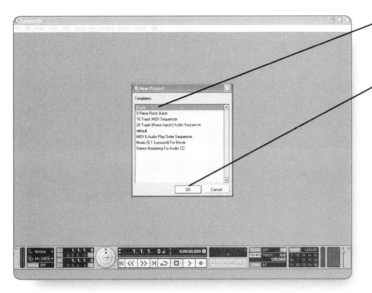

3. **Click** on **Empty**. The template will become highlighted.

4. **Click** on **OK**. The Select Directory dialog window will appear (Set Project folder for Macintosh users).

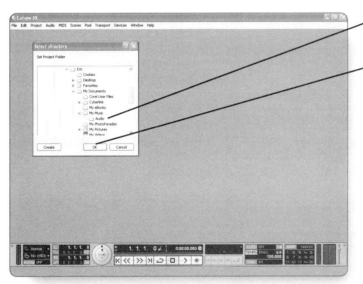

5. **Select** the **directory** in which you want to store the project.

6. **Click** on **OK**. The empty project will appear.

TIP

The Create Button

You can use the Create button in the Select Directory dialog window to create a new folder on your hard disk for the project. Macintosh users use the New Folder in the Set Project Folder Finder dialog window.

> ## NOTE
> ### Audio Directories
> For every project created, SX will create one more sub-directory labeled "Audio" in the directory in which you chose to store the project. This directory stores all audio recorded into the project.

> ## NOTE
> ### The Template Window
> When creating a new project, the template window will always appear. We'll take a closer look at working with these templates later in this chapter.

Making Project Settings

Now that you have a blank project loaded, let's look at how to make adjustments to the project settings. These changes will determine the sound quality and project length.

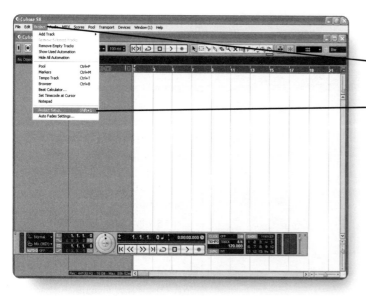

Start by opening the Project Settings dialog window.

1. Click on the **Project menu**. The Project menu will appear.

2. **Click** on **Project Setup**. The Project Settings dialog window will appear.

Adjusting the Sound Quality

One of the key settings you will want to adjust is sound quality.

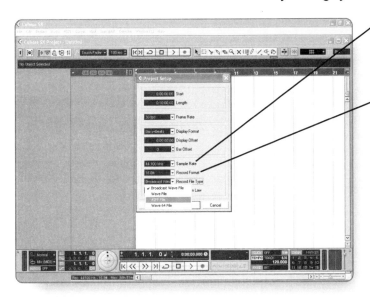

1. **Click** on the **Sample Rate drop-down menu**. Select the desired sample rate for the project.

2. **Click** on the **Record Format drop-down menu**. Select the desired bit rate (16, 24, or 32).

NOTE

Sample Rate and Record Format

As a general rule, the higher the sample and bit rates are, the better the sound quality will be. The available sample rates and bit rates are dependent on the audio card you are using. If, for example, your audio card does not support a 48KHz sample rate, this option will not be available (the same is true for Record Format). In addition, the higher the rates are, the larger the burden that is placed on your computer; I suggest that you experiment with these settings.

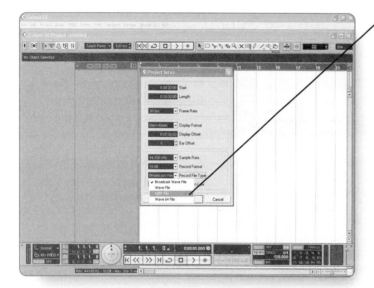

3. Click on the **Record File Type drop-down menu** to select the file type that will be used when recording audio. The default settings here are adequate (wave files for Windows users, and AIFF files for Mac OS X users).

Adjusting the Project Length

Next, we'll adjust the length of the project. By default, the project's length is set to ten minutes; however, if your project is going to be shorter than that, you'll want to adjust the length so that it is just a touch longer than your actual project length. For this exercise you'll change the project's length from ten minutes to five minutes.

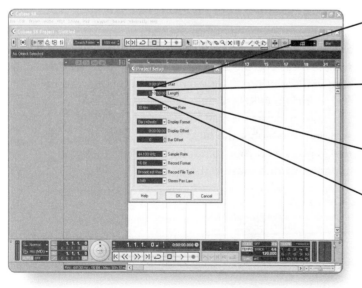

1. Click on **10** in the length field. The digits will become highlighted.

2. Type in **5**. The digits will read 05. The project is now five minutes long.

- Changing these digits will change the seconds of a project.

- Changing these digits will change the length in hours.

> **NOTE**
>
> **The Last Two Digits**
>
> The last two digits are reserved for specifying the number of frames per second (for example, thirty frames per second). These settings are usually used when synchronizing SX to another computer or to video gear. There is no need to change them unless you are working in one of the above situations, in which case consult SX's documentation. It should also be noted that you can set the number of frames per second in the Frame Rate field of the Project Setup window.

Working with Templates

Templates are a great way to save customized project settings, which will enable you to start new projects without having to readjust the settings.

Starting a Project Using Pre-Installed Templates

A few sample templates were installed with SX. We are going to use these templates to demonstrate how to create a new project with them.

Before you continue, you'll need to close the project created in the previous exercise. Do this by clicking on the X in the top-right corner of the project window.

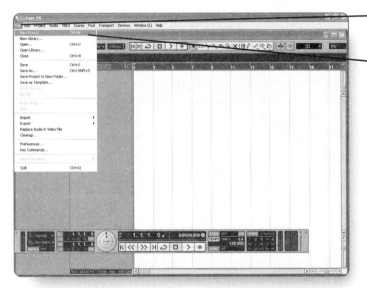

1. Click on the **File menu**. The File menu will appear.

2. Click on **New Project**. The New Project dialog window will appear.

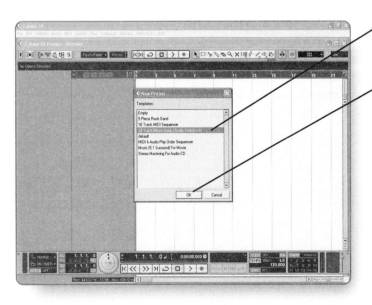

3. Click on **24 Track Audio Sequencer**. The template will become highlighted.

4. Click on **OK**. The Select directory dialog window will appear.

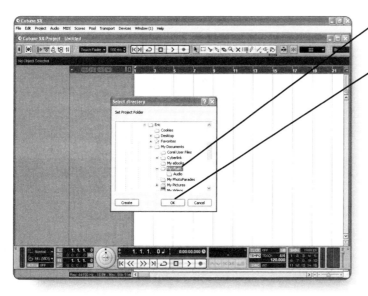

5. Select the **directory** in which you want to store the project.

6. Click on **OK**. A new project will appear with 24 audio tracks already added to the project.

Creating Your Own Custom Template

Next you'll alter the template you just loaded to create a template of your own. For your custom template, we are going to imagine that you are working with a five-piece rock band. You will set up the required number of tracks needed for each member (instrument) of the band, as well as rename the tracks for each.

Begin by removing unnecessary tracks.

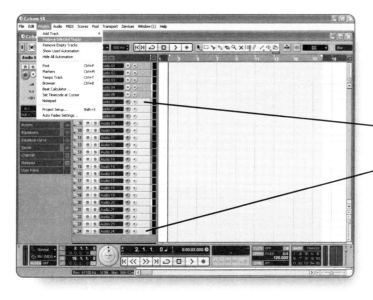

1. Click on **track 6**. The track will become highlighted.

2. Shift + click on **track 24**. All tracks from 6 to 24 will become highlighted.

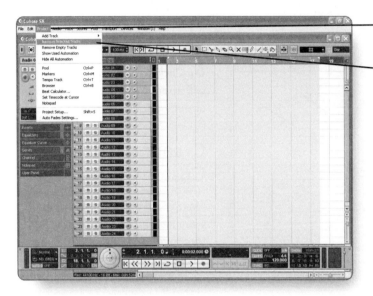

3. **Click** on the **Project menu**. The Project menu will appear.

4. **Click** on **Remove Selected Tracks**. Tracks 6 to 24 will be removed; only tracks 1 to 5 will remain.

TIP

Track Removal Shortcut

You can also remove selected tracks by right-clicking on the tracks and choosing "Remove Selected Tracks" from the pop-up menu.

Now we're going to rename the tracks for each instrument.

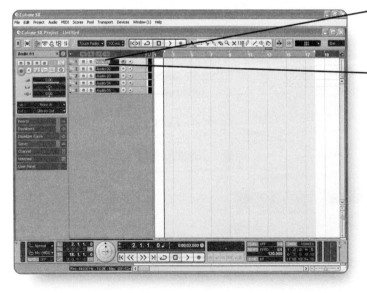

1. **Double-click** on **Audio 01** on track 1. The track's name (Audio 01) will become highlighted.

2. **Type** in **Drums** and **press Enter**. The track will now be named Drums.

Repeat these steps for tracks 2 through 5:

- Change Audio 02 to Guitar One
- Change Audio 03 to Guitar Two
- Change Audio 04 to Bass
- Change Audio 05 to Vocals

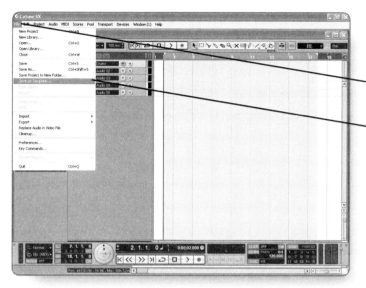

After the tracks have been renamed, let's save this as a new template.

1. Click on the **File menu**. The File menu will appear.

2. Click on **Save As Template**. The Save As Template dialog window will appear.

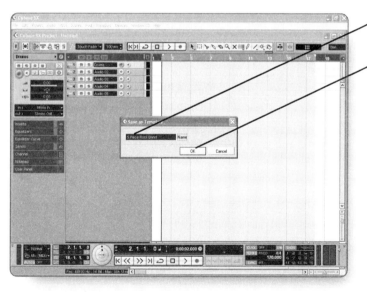

3. Type in **5 Piece Rock Band** in the Name field.

4. Click on **OK**. The template will be saved.

Now let's create a new project using our template.

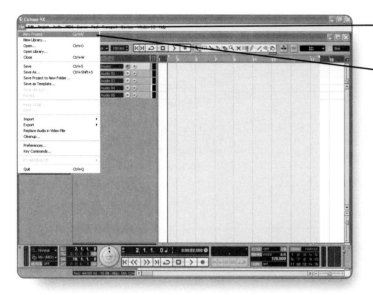

1. Click on the **File menu**. The File menu will appear.

2. Click on **New Project**. The New Project dialog window will appear.

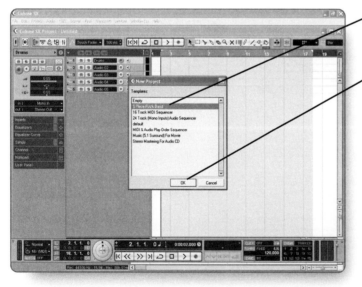

3. Click on **5 Piece Rock Band**. The template will become highlighted.

4. Click on **OK**. The Select Directory dialog window will appear. **Select** the **directory** in which you want to store the project and **click** on **OK**. The 5 Piece Rock Band template will now be loaded as the current project.

3

Recording Audio

Now that your computer is configured to run SX, and you are comfortable creating new projects and templates, we will begin adding material to a project. We'll begin with audio; perhaps one of the key elements of Cubase SX's popularity is its outstanding ability to record and edit audio material. To many, this is also the most attractive portion of the program. We'll begin by capturing audio to a track in SX.

In this chapter, you'll learn how to:

- Add and set up an audio track
- Work with input channels
- Record audio to your project

Adding and Setting Up an Audio Track

Before you can begin to record any audio to SX, you will need an audio track on which to record. You will also need to make adjustments to that audio track in order to capture a recording successfully.

Adding an Audio Track

Let's begin by adding an audio track to your project. You'll need to have an empty project open before moving on to the following exercise (refer to Chapter 2 for creating an empty project).

1. **Click** on the **Project menu**. The Project menu will appear.

2. **Click** on **Add Track**. The Add Track submenu will appear.

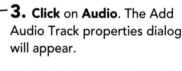

3. **Click** on **Audio**. The Add Audio Track properties dialog will appear.

In this dialog you will set the audio track's parameters.

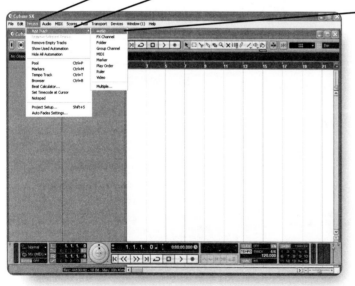

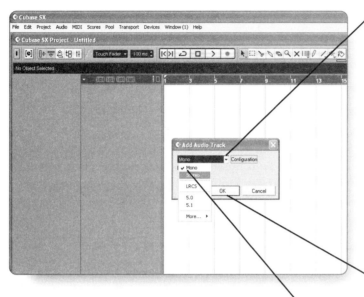

4. **Click** on the **Configuration drop-down menu**. The Audio Configuration menu will appear.

TIP

Adding Tracks Shortcut

You can also add an audio track, or any other track type, by right-clicking on the track list in the project window.

5a. **Click** on **OK**. A stereo track will be created in the project because the stereo option appears by default..

OR

5b. Select **Mono** and **click** on **OK**. A mono track will be added to the project.

NOTE

Choosing Tracks

To choose the correct type of track, mono or stereo, when creating an audio track, you'll need to think of the audio source you are recording. If it's a vocal from a microphone, then a mono track is sufficient; however, if you are recording a left and right output from a device such as a synthesizer or a vinyl record player, you should select stereo.

> ### NOTE
> #### Configuring Cubase SX
> In the Configuration drop-down menu are several other track options, such as LRS, 5.0, and 5.1; these settings are advanced settings for surround sound mixing. Because the purpose of this book is to get you familiar with fundamentals of SX, we are not going to cover surround sound mixing. If you are interested in learning more about surround sound, be sure to check out Robert Guerin's *Cubase SX/SL 3 Power!* also published by Course Technology.

> ### NOTE
> #### Track Display
> You can quickly determine whether a track is mono or stereo by looking at the display under the track name.

Setting the Track's Input and Enabling Track Monitoring

Before you can record anything, you will need to make sure that the audio track's input is set to the source of your audio (your microphone, for example). You will also need to monitor your input in order to hear what you are recording.

Setting the Track's Input

Now that you have an audio track added to the project, you will need to tell it which input of your audio card to record from. To set the input to an audio track, follow these steps.

1. **Click** on the **Show Inspector button**. The Inspector will open on the left side of the track list. The Inspector is part of the project window that allows you to adjust various track parameters (more on the Inspector in Chapter 5). You only need to follow this step if the Inspector is not already open.

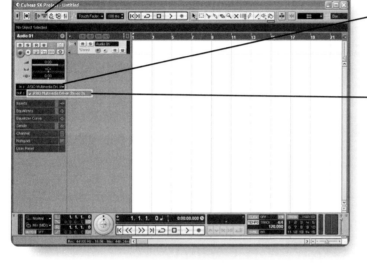

2. **Click** on the **In field** on the track's properties page. The Input drop-down menu will appear.

3. **Click** on the desired **Input**. The device will now be selected.

NOTE

Stereo Input

A stereo input consists of two mono input labels, left and right. Consult your audio card's documentation for more on your card's input configuration.

NOTE

Setting Track Input

A track's input can also be set in the input view of the mixer, which we'll look at in Chapter 9.

Monitoring

Monitoring is an important step when recording audio. Monitoring allows you to hear what the recorded audio will sound like before and during recording. One good reason for monitoring is to ensure that the input levels are not too high, which will cause harsh sounding digital distortion in your recording. Monitoring allows you to ensure that the volume is set to a comfortable level before recording.

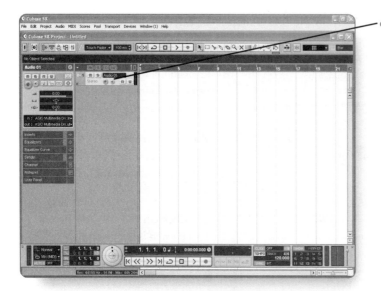

• Click on the small speaker icon on the track's properties page. The icon will turn orange indicating that monitoring is now activated. You will now be able to hear the audio source that is connected to the track's input.

Working with Input Channels (SX Version Only)

> ### NOTE
>
> **Input Channels**
>
> Inputs channels are only available with the SX version. SL users only need to make channel input settings when recording audio. Consult your SL documentation on setting up audio channels for recording in SL.

Input channels are special channels that give you more control of the inputs. With these channels you can adjust the input's level as well as add effects to the input which will be applied to the recorded material.

Adjusting Input Levels—Input Gain

Using the Input Gain function, you can adjust the input's level as the audio enters the input channel. This function can be useful if you have no other means of controlling the input level of your audio card.

NOTE

Using the Output Gain Knob

Generally the input level should always be set by the device that is feeding the audio to the audio card. That device could be the microphone preamp, keyboard, or guitar/bass amp (if recording directly from amp-line-out). So using the Output Gain knob of such analog equipment to set the recording level of the input channel is the recommended way to set input volumes.

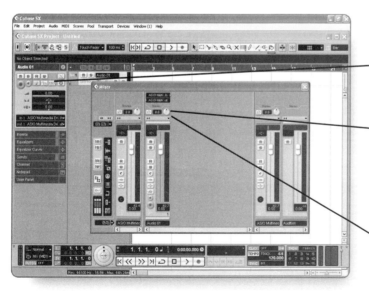

Begin by opening the mixer so you can see the input channels.

1. Click on the **Track Mixer icon** on the project window toolbar. The Mixer will appear.

2. Shift + click on the **Input Gain knob**.

3. Turn to the **right** to increase the inputs level. **Turn** to the **left** to decrease the level.

4. Ctrl + click on the **Input Gain knob**. The Input Gain will reset to zero.

Knob Controls to Faders

Many of the knob controls in Cubase can also be adjusted by using a fader as opposed to the knob control. Some users find

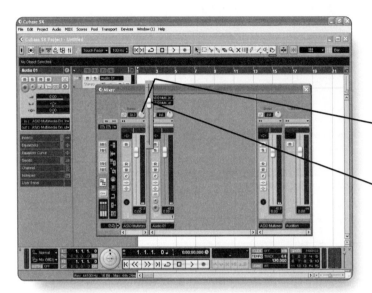

it easier and more accurate to control a parameter with a fader. To demonstrate this, let's adjust the Input Gain again using a fader control instead of the knob control.

1. **Alt + click** on the **Input Gain knob**. The Input Gain fader control will appear.

2. **Raise** the **fader** to increase the Input Gain level; **lower** the **fader** to reduce the level. The Input Gain knob control will also turn to reflect the changes.

TIP

Resetting Controls

Most of the controls and parameters in SX (for example, level knobs and faders) can be reset by Alt + clicking (Control + clicking for Macintosh users) on the parameter.

CAUTION

The 0db Point

When recording, try to have the level of your audio as high as possible without going over the 0db point. Going over 0db will produce digital distortion such as clicks and pops in the recorded material. Be sure the input is not going over 0db *before* adjusting the Input Gain control.

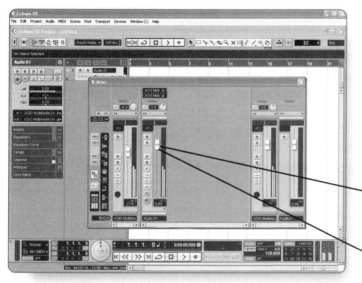

Adjusting the Recording Levels

Once you have set the input levels, you can then use the channel's volume fader to control the output level of the channel; this in turn will control the level of the recording.

1. Raise the **fader** to increase the output level of the input channel.

2. Lower the **fader** to decrease the output level.

NOTE

Red Light Indicator

As with input levels, the output of the channel should not go over 0db. On the left side, near the bottom of the input channel's fader is a small circular LED labeled with a C. If this button turns red, this is an indication that the output of the channel is going over 0db. If the light becomes red, you'll need to manually reset it by clicking on it.

TIP

Using the Output Level

In most cases you will want to control the input channel's level with the output control of the source you are recording and leave the Output Fader at its default position of 0db. However, when working with effects in the input channel (effects in the input channel are covered later in this chapter), the output of the channel may change. Use the output level to compensate for the effect's level changes.

Recording Audio

Now that you have made all the necessary settings to your audio track, we are closer to getting audio into your project—just a few more settings to make.

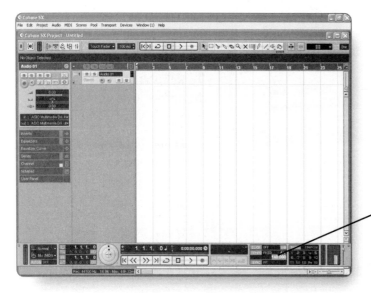

Setting the Song's Tempo

Before you record any audio, you need to set the tempo of your project. I highly recommend that you set the tempo before recording; if you try to change the tempo after recording, the audio may not match the tempo.

1. **Click** on **Tempo** in the transport bar. The Tempo setting will change to Fixed.

NOTE

The Tempo Track

By default, the tempo setting is set to Track. The tempo track does not appear in the project window but it allows you to make tempo changes throughout the song. For these exercises we will be using a fixed tempo. For more information on using the tempo track, consult SX's documentation.

2. **Click** on the **Tempo value** (by default a project is set to 120 bpm). The value will become highlighted.

3. **Type** the desired **tempo** (for example, 140) and **press Enter**. The tempo will now be set to your desired speed.

> **NOTE**
>
> **Problems Changing Tempo**
>
> If you are typing in a new tempo value, but the setting remains at 120, you need to verify that the tempo is set to Fixed and not Track.

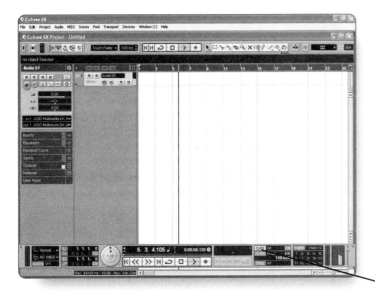

Using the Metronome

If you have ever taken piano lessons, you know what a metronome is. For those who don't know, a metronome is a device that produces a small clicking sound on every beat. The purpose of the metronome is to ensure that your timing while playing is correct to the project's tempo. Let's begin by enabling the metronome:

1. **Click** on **Click** on the transport panel. The metronome will be enabled.

2. **Click** on the **Play button** on the transport panel. The project will begin to play back. You'll hear a click sound on every quarter beat (the first beat of each bar is accented).

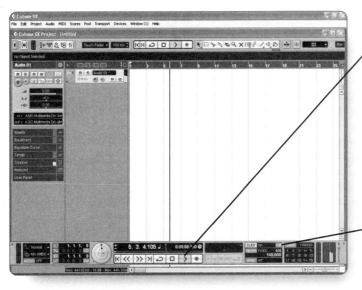

Now set the metronome so that it gives you a two-bar count-in before recording starts.

3. **Click** on the **Pre-count button** on the transport panel. The two-bar count-in will be activated.

> **TIP**
>
> **Setting Count-In Only**
>
> It is possible to have the metronome provide you with a count-in only and not click throughout the playback. Simply activate the Pre-Count feature and disable Click. This may be helpful if you are recording over the top of audio tracks, such as drums, when a metronome is not needed.

Recording—Using Punch In and Punch Outs

Okay, we're ready to begin recording audio. Not only are you going to learn how to record audio, you are going to learn to record using a punch in and a punch out. Punch ins and punch outs allow SX to begin or stop recording automatically when the project playback cursor reaches a predetermined timing point.

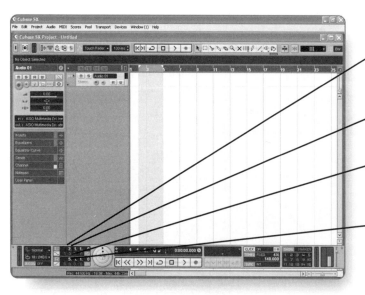

Recording

1. **Click** on the **first digit** on the left locator position. The digit will become highlighted.

2. **Enter** the value **2**. **Press Enter**.

3. **Click** on the **first digit** on the right locator position. The digit will become highlighted.

4. **Enter** the value **5**. **Press Enter/Return**.

Along the top of the project window, you will see a blue highlighted section starting at bar 2 and ending at bar 5. In between these two points is where the recording will take place.

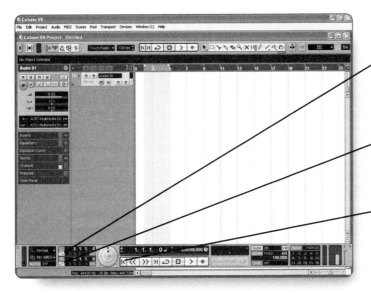

Now you will need to activate the punch in.

5. **Click** on the **Punch In button** under the L in the transport panel. The punch in point is now active.

6. **Click** on the **Punch Out button**. Punch out will be activated.

7. **Click** on the **Return to Zero button**. This will bring the project cursor back to the start position.

TIP

Track Default Name

When SX names the file for the recording, it will use the track name as its base. Before recording it would be a good idea to rename the track.

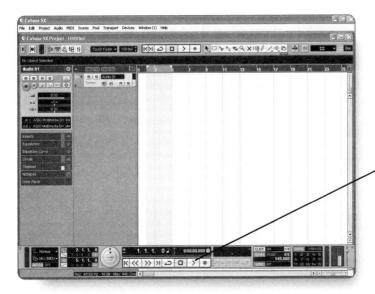

8. **Click** on the **Play button**. The project will begin playing. When the project cursor reaches bar 2, recording will begin. While recording is taking place, a gray box containing the audio waveform display will be drawn behind the project cursor; this will indicate that the audio is being successfully recorded to the track. When the cursor reaches bar 5, recording will automatically stop; however, playback will continue until you click the Stop button.

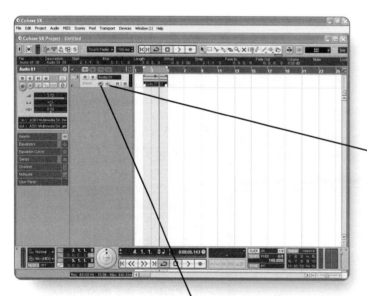

Listening to the Recording

In order to hear the audio you just recorded to the track, you'll need to reverse some of the settings you made prior to recording.

1. **Click** on the **Monitoring button** on the audio track to disable input monitoring. When input monitoring is enabled on an audio track, you will be able to hear audio only from input that is connected to the track and not the audio that was recorded to it.

2. **Click** on the **Rec Enable button**. The track will be disarmed for recording so audio cannot be recorded to the track.

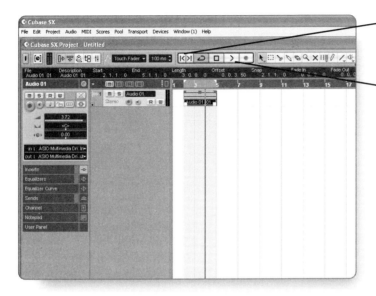

3. Click on the **Return to Zero button**. The project cursor will return to the start.

4. Click on the **Play button**. The project will begin playback.

Recording with Effects

Until the release of SX 2, effects in Cubase could be used only on pre-recorded material. These effects now can be applied to the input channels so that they are then applied to the recordings. Recording with effects is a personal choice; many users prefer to apply effects after recording so that they're not committed to them. Some, on the other hand, prefer to record with the effects.

Now we are going to apply a simple reverb effect to the input channel. The reverb will be applied to the recording.

1. Click on the **Track Mixer icon** in the project window toolbar. The Mixer will appear.

2. Click on the **E button** on the input channel. This will open the Input Channel Settings dialog window.

3. Click on **Effect Insert Slot One**. A drop-down menu of all available plug-in effects will appear.

4. Click on **Reverb**. The Reverb submenu will appear.

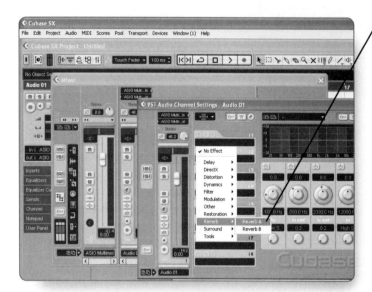

5. Click on **Reverb A**. The Reverb Effect dialog window will appear where you can adjust the settings for the reverb.

NOTE

Plug-In Effects

You can learn more about applying effects in Chapter 10. For more information on the available plug-ins, consult SX's documentation.

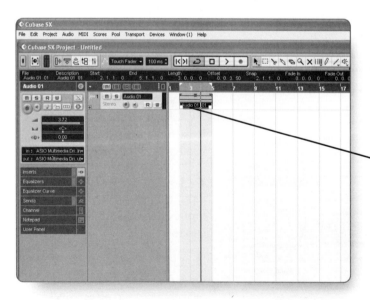

Now we are going to record audio to your project again. This time the reverb will be applied to the recorded material. First you will need to clear the recorded material from the previous exercise.

1. Click on the **audio event** that you recorded to your audio track. The event will become highlighted.

2. Press Delete on your keyboard. The event will be removed from the project.

NOTE

Removing Audio

Removing audio from the project does not delete the audio file from your hard disk; the file can be removed permanently by using the Pool (more on the Pool in Chapter 14).

Now let's record. For this exercise, we are going to assume that you still have your punch out point set to bar 5.

1. Click on the **Record Enable button** for the audio track if it is not already selected. The track will be enabled for recording.

2. Click on the **Punch In button** if it is not already selected. Punch in will become active.

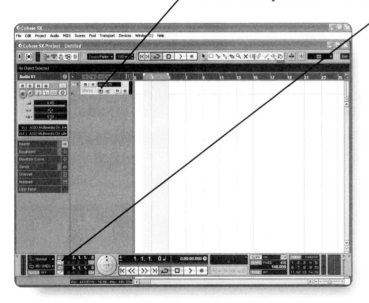

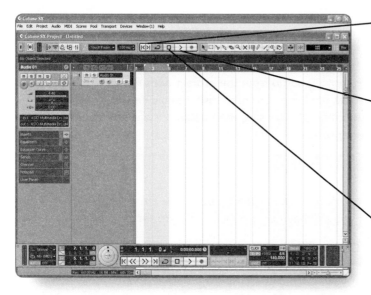

3. Click on the **Return to Zero button** from the transport panel. The project position will return to the start of the project.

4. Click on the **Play button**. SX will begin to play back. When the cursor reaches bar 2, recording will begin. When the project position cursor reaches bar 5, recording will stop.

5. Click **Stop** to end the process.

6. Click on **Return to Zero**. The project position will return to the start of the project.

7. Click on the **Play button**. The project will begin playback, and you will hear the audio that you just recorded.

4

Recording MIDI

What is MIDI? How is it different from audio? MIDI (an acronym for Musical Instrument Digital Interface) is a protocol that allows computers to control synthesizers and allows synthesizers to control one another. MIDI carries instructions—like what notes were pressed, how hard they were pressed, and how long they were held. Think of MIDI as a digital (and greatly enhanced) form of the old paper rolls used in player pianos. MIDI files can be acquired (from several media sources such as the Internet) or created in a MIDI application—in this case SX.

In this chapter, you'll learn how to:

- Load tutorial projects
- Add a MIDI track to your project
- Connect the inputs and outputs of a MIDI track
- Record MIDI to the project

Loading the Tutorial Project

In this chapter, we will begin to work with the tutorial projects. You can download the projects at **www.courseptr.com/downloads**. Once downloaded, extract the zipped files to a folder on your hard disk.

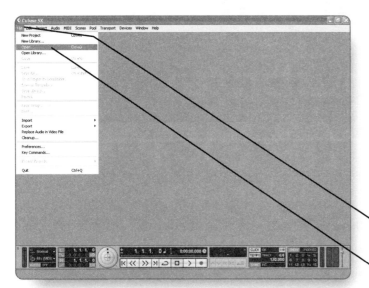

TIP

Download the Tutorials

Since there are several tutorial projects that accompany this book, it would be a good idea to download all the tutorials prior to continuing.

1. Click on the **File menu**. The File menu will appear.

2. Click on **Open**. The Open Project dialog will appear.

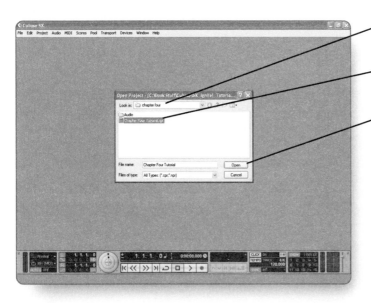

3. Navigate to the **folder** in which you extracted the zip file.

4. Click on the **Chapter Four Tutorial project file**.

5. Click on **Open**. The project will be loaded into Cubase SX. A dialog box called Pending Connections may appear. If this is the case simply click OK.

Adding a MIDI Track

In this chapter, you will learn how to record to a MIDI track; however, you'll first need to create a track to record the MIDI to. We are going to be working with an empty project for the following exercises (refer to Chapter 2 on how to create a new empty project).

1. **Click** on the **Project menu**. The Project menu will appear.

2. **Click** on **Add Track**. The Add Track submenu will appear.

3. **Click** on **MIDI**. A MIDI track will be added to the project.

TIP

Adding Tracks Shortcut

Remember, you can also add a track by right-clicking on the track list and choosing the track type from the pop-up menu.

Connecting a MIDI Track's Inputs and Outputs

To hear what is recorded to a MIDI track, you'll need to connect the track's output to a MIDI device. This device could be an external synthesizer, drum machine, or even a VST instrument. For this exercise we'll connect the track to a VST instrument that is already loaded in the tutorial project (we'll be taking a closer look at loading VST instruments in Chapter 8).

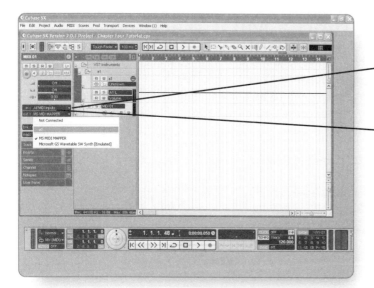

Connect your MIDI controller to the track's input.

1. Click on the **In drop-down menu**. The list of available inputs will appear.

2. Click on the **input** that is connected to your MIDI controller.

TIP

Rename Inputs and Outputs

If you find that the default names of your MIDI inputs and outputs are confusing, remember you can rename them in the Device Setup dialog. Refer to Chapter 1 to learn how to do this.

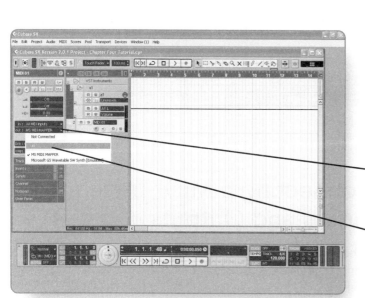

Connect the track's output to the VST instrument A1.

3. Click on the **Output drop-down menu**. The list of available outputs will appear.

4. Click on **A1** from the drop-down menu. The track's output will now be connected to the A1 synthesizer.

By playing your MIDI controller, you should hear the A1 (which is a bass guitar patch). This is because the controller is connected to the MIDI track's inputs, and the track's output is connected to the A1.

> **NOTE**
>
> **Input and Output Names**
>
> The available inputs and outputs depend on the MIDI hardware installed on your computer. The list may differ from what is shown here.

> **NOTE**
>
> **Selecting MIDI Output**
>
> If you want to use the sounds of an external MIDI keyboard or sound module, you need to select the output that is connected to your external device from the Output drop-down menu.

Recording MIDI

Now that your track is connected to the A1 VST instrument and can be heard when you play your controller, the next step is to record. We are going to use the same punch in and punch out options that we used when we recorded audio in Chapter 3.

Setting the Punch In and Out Times—Locators

In Chapter 3, we entered the punch in and out times manually. Here you will learn to set the punch in and out points by adjusting the locators. There are two locators L (left) and R (right); these locators are used for punch in and out times as well as for setting up a recording and playback cycle (more on working with cycles later in this chapter).

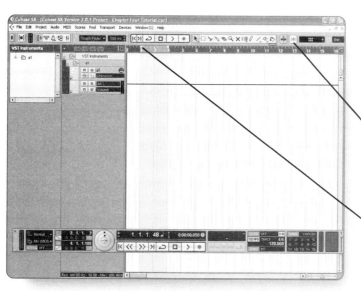

1. Click on **Snap On/Off**. This will enable snapping. Snapping ensures that the locators will be placed only at the beginning of a bar.

2. Move your **cursor** to the upper half on bar 2 of the project window's ruler. The cursor will become a pencil.

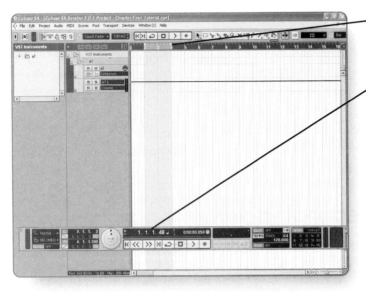

3. Click and drag to **bar 4**. The left locator will be set to bar 2 and the right to bar 4.

The locator times reflect the changes made by drawing in the locators.

Now activate punch in and out.

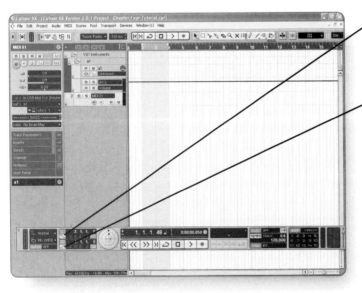

1. Click on the **Punch In button** on the transport panel. The button will highlight, indicating that punch in is enabled.

2. Click on the **Punch Out button** on the transport panel. The button will highlight to indicate that punch out is activated.

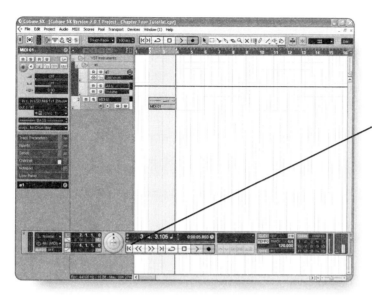

Recording

Now you are going to record a MIDI performance to the MIDI track.

1. **Click** on the **Return to Zero button** to ensure that the project cursor is set to the beginning.

TIP

Jumping to the Beginning

Pressing the "," (comma) key on your keyboard will return the project cursor to the beginning.

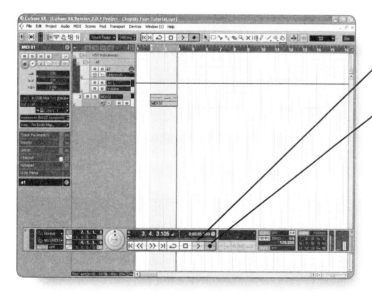

2. **Click** on the **Play button**. The project will begin playback.

3. **Click** on the **Stop button**. The playback will stop.

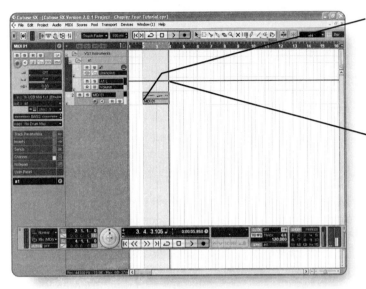

When the project cursor reaches bar 2, the Record button will engage and recording will begin. Play your MIDI controller. What you play will be recorded to the track.

When the cursor hits bar 4, the Record button will disengage and recording will stop (playback will continue until you click on stop).

NOTE

The Gray Box

As when recording audio, a gray box will be drawn behind the cursor during recording. This box will contain the notes you played from your MIDI controller. If you did not play your MIDI controller during the recording, the box will be removed automatically from the track after recording has stopped. If you did in fact play your controller and the box is still being removed automatically, then you will need to double-check that the track's input is set to the same input your controller is connected to.

Cycle Recording—Record Modes

Cycle recording automatically loops the portion of the project between the left and right locators. This is helpful in a few ways. It allows you to play the part you are recording several times until you feel that you got the best performance possible without stopping the project. And if you're not a good keyboard player, cycle recording will allow you to build the part by playing one piece or note at a time, adding to it with each cycle.

Overwrite Mode—Multiple Takes

Let's begin by using the Cycle mode to play a part several times until you capture a performance you are satisfied with. To do this, you'll use the Overwrite Cycle mode. When using this mode each cycle will overwrite the previous cycle's recording.

1. Click on the **Cycle Record mode drop-down menu** on the transport panel. A drop-down menu will appear.

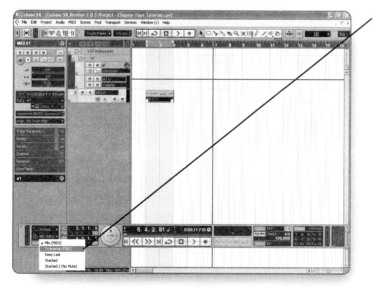

2. Click on **Overwrite (MIDI)**. The Cycle mode will be set to Overwrite.

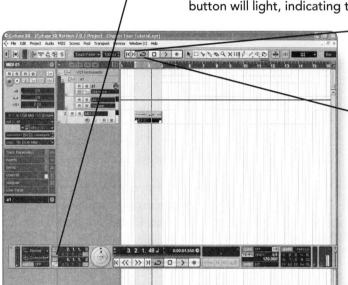

3. **Click** on the **Punch In button** on the transport panel. The button will light, indicating that punch in is enabled.

4. **Click** on the **Return to Zero button** on the transport panel. The project cursor will return to the beginning.

5. **Click** on the **Cycle button**. Cycle mode will be enabled.

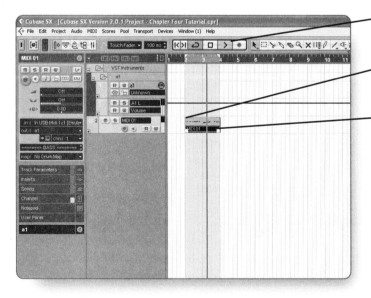

6. **Click** on the **Play button**. The project will begin playback.

When the cursor reaches bar 2, recording will begin.

When the cursor reaches bar 4, the project cursor will cycle back to bar 2 and continue recording. This will continue until you click on the Stop button.

CAUTION

Stopping Cycle Recording

To stop cycle recording, you will have to click the Stop button; if you stop the cycle while the cursor is in between the locators, the last complete cycle will be the final take. Therefore, when you are satisfied with the performance, be sure not to play any additional notes until you have clicked on the Stop button.

Mix Mode—Building a Part

Now we will use the Mix mode with cycle recording to allow you to build a part one piece or note at a time. When using this mode, each cycle will add the notes you play to the previous cycle (as opposed to overwriting them).

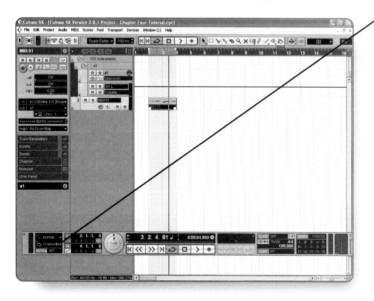

1. **Click** on the **Cycle Record mode drop-down menu** on the transport panel.

2. Click on **Mix (MIDI)**. The Cycle mode will be set to Mix.

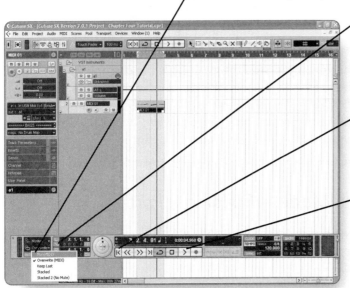

3. Click on the **Punch In button** on the transport panel if it is not already enabled. The button will highlight, indicating that punch in is enabled.

4. Click on the **Return to Zero button** on the transport panel. The project cursor will return to the beginning.

5. Click on the **Play button**. The project will begin playback.

Again when the cursor hits bar 2, recording will begin, and when it reaches bar 4, it will cycle back to bar 2. During the cycle, play one note of your part on your MIDI controller. With each cycle, play the next note of the part until you have played all parts; then click on stop to end the recording.

5

Arranging in the Project Window

The project window is the heart of Cubase SX. Up to this point, you have worked with the project window to add audio and MIDI tracks, and to make some adjustments to their settings. The project window is also where you will edit the arrangement of your projects. Working with blocks of audio and MIDI, you can move, resize, copy, paste, and more, to build the foundation of your song in minutes. The project window also provides several tools that will help you with your workflow and navigation.

In this chapter, you'll learn how to:

- Navigate the project window
- Arrange and edit audio and MIDI in the project window

Navigating the Project Window

Let's begin by taking a quick tour of the project window and the common components that will improve your workflow, which simply means the steps you take when working with projects. Cubase SX provides several ways to perform many of its functions. Each user generally develops her own way of working with Cubase. The key is to establish a workflow that does not hinder your creative process.

For the exercises in this chapter you will need to download and open the Chapter 5 tutorial project from **www.courseptr.com/ downloads**. If necessary, refer to Chapter 4 on how to open tutorial projects. If you don't have access to the tutorial files, don't worry, you can always apply these instructions to any existing events that you have recorded.

Track Inspector

The Inspector is a set of screens that are positioned to the left of the track listing. Consisting of seven individual windows, the Inspector allows you to control various settings for each track. Let's take a look at how to open the Inspector as well as open the windows.

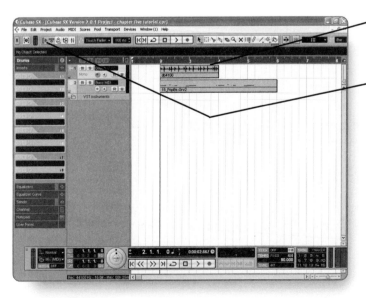

1. **Click** on the **Drums audio track**. The track will become highlighted.

2. **Click** on the **Show Inspector button** if the Inspector is not already open. The Inspector window will appear to the left of the track list. By default, the Inspector will display the track properties for the drum track (we'll be looking at these properties in Chapter 9). Now we are going to look at how to change the dialog window.

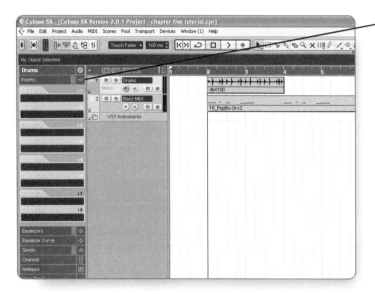

3. Click on the **Show Active Inserts button** beside the word Inserts. The Insert menu will expand. The Insert menu is where you would apply an Insert effect on a track (more on using Inserts in Chapter 9).

NOTE

Inspector Window Shortcut

To view any of the Inspector dialog windows, simply click the icon beside the name of the menu you want to expand.

NOTE

Alternative Methods for Opening Inspector Dialog Windows

As mentioned earlier, there are several ways to perform the same function; this is also true of the various inspector dialog windows. These windows are used when applying EQ and effects, which we'll be looking at in the mixing portion of the book starting in Chapter 9.

Zooming the Project

When working with a project you may want to take a closer look at the parts on the tracks—or perhaps the opposite—you may want to see the project in whole, viewing all of its contents. To change how you look at the project, you will use SX's zooming features. SX offers several ways to zoom in and out of the project. We are going to look at some of the common ways to perform zooming.

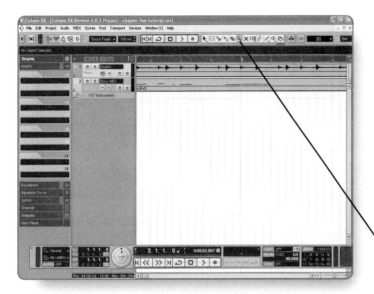

Vertical Zooming

To control how much of the project's length is viewable in the project window you will use one of the various vertical zooming methods.

The Zoom Tool

The first method for vertical zooming is to use the Zoom tool.

1. **Click** on the **Zoom tool** on the toolbar. The mouse pointer will become a magnifying glass.

NOTE

Magnifying Glass Position

The mouse pointer will be a magnifying glass only when placed over the project window.

TIP

Tool Selection Shortcut

You can also select a tool by right-clicking anywhere in the project window and selecting the desired tool from the pop-up menu.

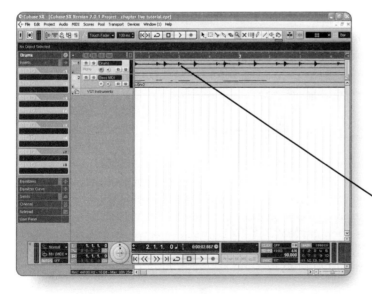

2. **Click and drag** over the **drum part** on the drum track. The project window will zoom to size on the drum part.

Zooming with the Ruler

Perhaps the quickest and easiest way to vertically zoom the project is to use the ruler. The ruler lies across the top of the project and displays timing information.

1. Place the **mouse pointer** over the lower half of the ruler.

NOTE

Mouse Placement Doesn't Matter

It does not matter which tool is currently selected, since the mouse pointer will be placed on the ruler and outside of the project window.

2. Click and drag the **mouse** downward. As you drag the mouse the project will zoom in.

3. Drag the **mouse** upwards. The project will zoom out.

NOTE

Changing Focus Point

The zoom will use the position of the playback cursor as its center focus point. It is possible to move the cursor to the left or right while zooming in and out, allowing you to change this focal point while zooming.

Project Overview

The overview is like a bird's-eye view over the entire project. Use this view to select a portion of the project you want to view in the project window.

1. **Click** on the **Show Overview button**. The overview window will appear above the ruler of the project window. In the

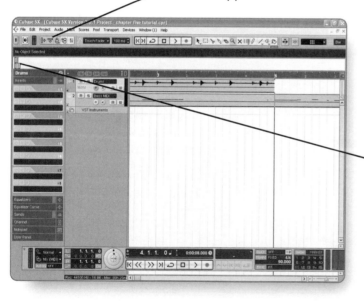

overview window you will be able to see the entire project with a blue box around the project's contents (the contents are the gray sections). The contents within the blue box are what will be displayed in the project window.

2. **Place** your **mouse cursor** at the right edge of the blue box. The cursor will become a double-sided arrow.

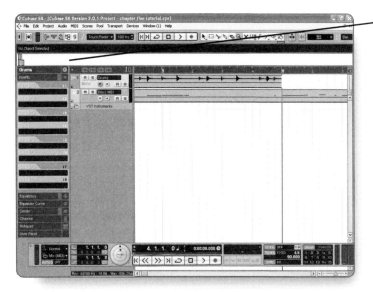

3. **Drag** the **right edge of the blue box** to the right. The project window will zoom out. Drag the box to the left; the project will zoom in.

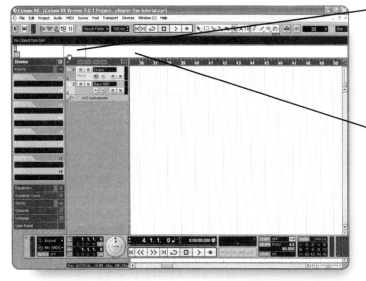

4. **Place** the **pointer** over the bottom half of the overview window. The pointer will become a Hand tool; this tool is used to change the position of the blue box within the project.

5. **Click and drag** the **box** to the right. The project window will scroll through the project.

NOTE

Pan with the Hand

Although the Hand tool in the overview window does not actually zoom in or out on the project, it does allow you to quickly change the portion of the project that is displayed in the project window.

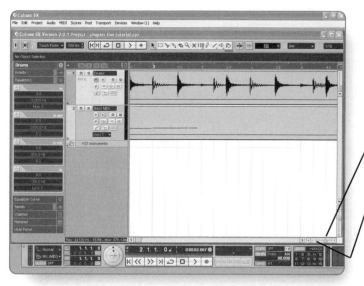

The Vertical Zoom Slider

The zoom slider is a simple slider for zooming in and out of the project. It is located at the bottom-right corner of the project window.

1. **Click and drag** the **vertical zoom slider** to the right. The project will zoom out.

2. **Drag** to the **left**. The project will zoom in.

Horizontal Zooming

Horizontal zooming allows you to control the horizontal size of the tracks in the Project window. This can be helpful when you want to get a clearer view of the contents on a certain track or tracks.

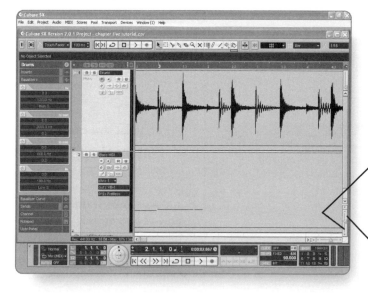

The Horizontal Zoom Slider

The horizontal zoom slider works in the same manner as the vertical slider; however, the slider will zoom in and out horizontally.

1. **Click and drag** the **vertical zoom slider** downwards. The horizontal width of the tracks will decrease.

2. **Drag** the **slider** upward. The horizontal track width will increase.

Zooming Individual Tracks

It is possible to increase or decrease the horizontal width of an individual track. This could be helpful when you want a more detailed view of a specific track.

1. Place your **mouse cursor** over the line that divides the drum track and bass track. The cursor will change to a line with an arrow above and below the line.

2. Drag the **line** upwards. The drum track's horizontal width will decrease. Drag it down and the width will increase.

Zooming to Selected Parts or Events

Zooming to selected parts or events will allow you to zoom both vertically and horizontally on a particular part in the project window. This will allow you to quickly zoom into a part that you want to edit or simply take a closer look at.

To demonstrate, we are going to zoom the drum event.

1. Click on the **drum part**. The event will become highlighted.

2. Click on the **Edit menu**. The Edit menu will appear.

3. Click on **Zoom**. The Zoom submenu will appear.

4. Click on **Zoom to Selection**. The project window will zoom in on the drum event.

TIP

Zooming to Selected Shortcut

You can also use the key command Alt + S (Windows) or Command + S (Macintosh) to zoom into the selected event(s) or part(s).

NOTE

Zooming to Selected Alternative

In the Edit > Zoom menu there is also the Zoom to Selected (Horiz.) option; this option will zoom only the selected event or part horizontally.

TIP

Zooming Shortcut

It is easy to zoom in too far; a quick way to zoom out to the full project is to use the Shift + F key command. This command will zoom out to view the entire project, both vertically and horizontally.

Arranging with the Project Window

Now we are going to begin performing edits to the tutorial project, which should already be loaded. The project consists of two tracks: One track is an audio recording of a drum kit; the other is a MIDI track playing the A1 VST instrument. Typically, the project window is used for building the arrangement of your song (verse, chorus, bridge, and so on); here you will learn how to move sections of the project around as well as edit them to complete a simple arrangement. As you work your way through the following steps it would be a good idea to play back the project to hear the changes that you have made.

Copying Audio Events and MIDI Parts

The first thing you will notice is that the drum audio event is only two bars long, whereas the bass is four bars. We will copy the two bars of the drum audio event so that it will match the length of the bass part.

1. While **holding** the **Alt key** for Windows (**Command key** for Macintosh), **click and drag** the **drum audio event** so that the beginning of the audio event lines up at bar 4.

2. **Release** the **mouse**. The audio event will now be copied to bar 4; now there are two drum audio events, which together equal the same length as the bass part.

CAUTION

Release the Mouse Button First

When releasing the mouse button, you must still be holding the Alt/Command key. If you're not, the part or audio event will not copy; it will be moved to the point where you released the mouse instead.

Now that the parts or audio events are equal in length, let's make both the MIDI parts and audio events eight bars long.

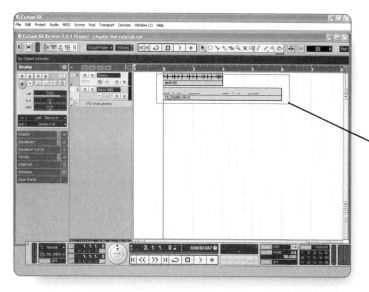

1. **Click and drag** your **mouse pointer** around both the drum and bass parts. As you drag, a marquee will appear; anything this marquee touches will be selected when you release the mouse button.

TIP

Part Selection Shortcut

You could also use the key command Ctrl + A
(Windows)/Command + A (Macintosh) to select all the
parts on the project window.

---

2. **Alt + Click** (Windows)/**Command + Click** (Macintosh) on
the selected parts and events.

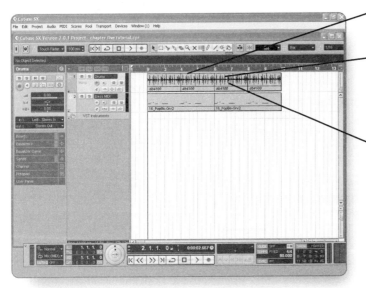

3. **Drag** the **parts** so that they
start at bar 6.

4. **Release** the **mouse button**.
The selected parts and events
will now be copied to start at
bar 6.

5. You can click in any blank
area to deselect the parts.

NOTE

Zooming Out

Depending on your screen
resolution and zoom
settings, you may need to
zoom out of the project to
view all the parts of the
project.

Removing Audio Events or MIDI Parts

Next, we'll remove a portion of the drum track to create a
break.

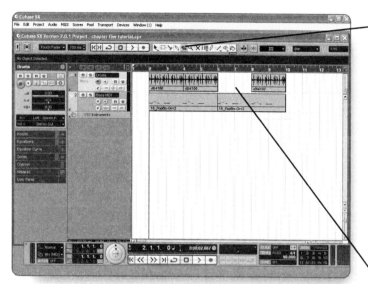

1. Click on the **Eraser tool**. The mouse cursor will become an eraser.

TIP

Alternative Eraser Tool Selection

Remember, you can also right-click on the project and select the Eraser tool from the pop-up menu.

---

2. Click on the **drum audio event** between bars 6 and 8. The audio event will be removed.

TIP

Part Removal Alternative

You can also remove parts and audio events from the project window by selecting the part or audio event using the Selection tool and pressing Delete.

Splitting and Moving Audio Events and MIDI Parts

Between bars 6 and 8 there is a small break in the drums so that only the bass part plays; next, we are going to move the drum and bass parts that start after the break to start one beat earlier.

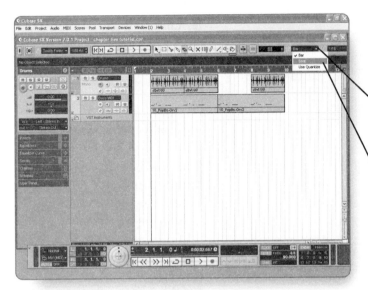

We need to begin by splitting the bass part at bar 8 so that we can move only a portion of the part.

1. **Click** on the **Grid Type menu** from the toolbar. The Grid Type drop-down menu will appear.

2. **Click** on **Beat** from the drop-down menu.

NOTE

Snapping to Grid

The grid allows you to move, copy, or split a part or an audio event to an exact note or bar position. You can set the grid to snap to Bar, Beat, or Use Quantize (more on Quantize later in this chapter).

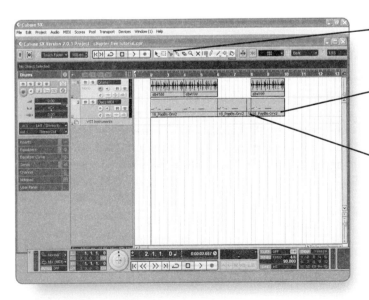

3. **Click** on the **Split tool**. Your mouse cursor will become a pair of scissors (the Split tool).

4. **Click** on the **bass part** at bar 8. The bass part will be split in two at bar 8.

5. **Click** on the **bass part** again at beat 4 of bar 7. The bass part will be split again.

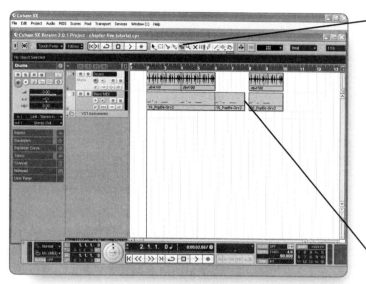

6. Click on the **Eraser tool**. Your cursor will become the Eraser tool.

TIP

Tool Selection Shortcut

Reminder—you can select a tool by right-clicking in the project window and selecting the desired tool.

7. Click on the **bass part** between beat 4 of bar 7 and beat 1 of bar 8. The audio event will be removed from the project.

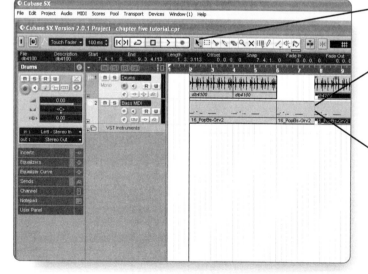

8. Click on the **Selection tool** from the toolbar. The pointer will become an arrow.

9. Click and drag the **mouse** over both the drum and bass parts between bars 8 and 10. The parts will become selected.

10. Click on the **drum audio event** and drag it to beat 4 of bar 7. The event will move to start on beat 4 of bar 7.

NOTE

Parts Move Together

When both parts are selected, it does not matter which part you drag; both parts will move to the desired location.

Gluing Events and Parts Together

Now we are going to copy the drum audio event to begin again at bar 10; however, we want to copy four bars of the drum audio event. To do this we are going to copy four bars of the drum audio event as well as create a new four-bar piece.

1. Click on the **Glue tool**. Your cursor will become the Glue tool.

2. Click on the **first drum audio event**. The audio event will be glued together with the drum audio event to the right to form a new part.

CAUTION

Look to the Right

When using the Glue tool, whichever part or audio event you click on will become glued to the part or audio event to the right only; be careful to click on the correct part or audio event you want to glue.

NOTE

Creating Audio Parts

When you glue two or more audio events together, the multiple events will become a part—more on audio events and parts comparisons in Chapter 6.

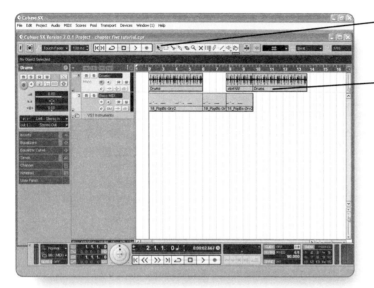

3. Click on the **Selection tool**. The pointer will become an arrow.

4. Alt + Click (Windows)/ **Command + Click** (Macintosh) on the **drum part** starting on bar 2 and drag it to bar 10.

CAUTION

Release the Mouse Button First

Remember to release the mouse button while still holding the Alt or Command key when copying parts or events.

NOTE

Gluing MIDI

In the previous example we glued two audio events together; the same can be done to MIDI parts as well.

Resizing Events and Parts

Now when you play back the project, the drums will stop at beat 4 of bar 9 and begin again at bar 10; however, when the drums stop on beat 4 of bar 9, there is a double kick drum that really doesn't match the one-beat break before the drums start again. We are going to remove the double kick by resizing the audio event.

We'll start by zooming in on the part we are going to edit.

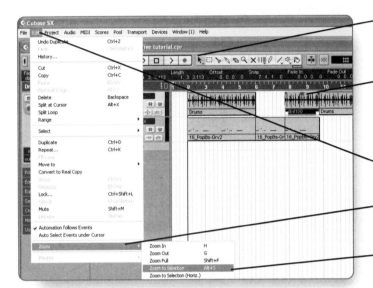

1. **Click** on the **Selection tool**. The pointer will become an arrow.

2. **Click** on the **drum audio event** that starts on beat 4 of bar 7. The audio event will become highlighted.

3. **Click** on the **Edit menu**. The Edit menu will appear.

4. **Click** on **Zoom**. The Zoom submenu will appear.

5. **Click** on **Zoom to Selection**. The project window will zoom in on the drum audio event.

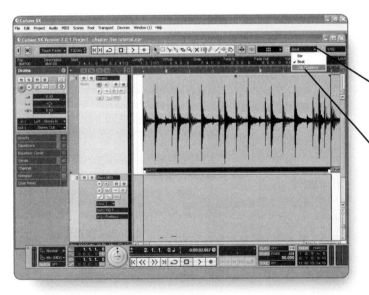

Now let's edit the double kick. We'll start by setting the grid size.

1. **Click** on the **Grid Type menu**. The Grid Type drop-down menu will appear.

2. **Click** on **Use Quantize**. The grid will be set to follow the Quantize values.

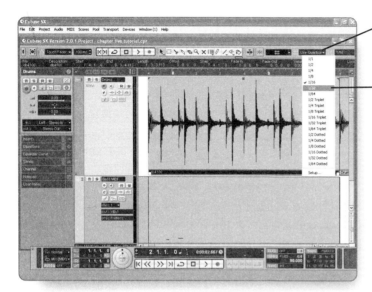

3. **Click** on the **Quantize Type menu**. The Quantize Type drop-down menu will appear.

4. **Click** on **1/32 Note**. The Quantize size will be set to a 32nd note.

NOTE

Quantize vs. Grid

Quantize allows you to move, resize, and split contents both in the project window and the editor windows to an exact note position, just as the grid does; however, the grid allows you to move, resize, and split only to a bar or beat. Quantize allows you to use smaller note sizes such as 8th and 16th notes.

Now let's resize the drum audio event.

5. **Click and drag** the **right handle** of the audio event to the left. As you drag, you will notice that the audio event is "snapping" to every 32nd note position (as we set in the Quantize type in step 4).

6. **Drag** the **event handle** until it snaps three times. The double kick drum will be removed.

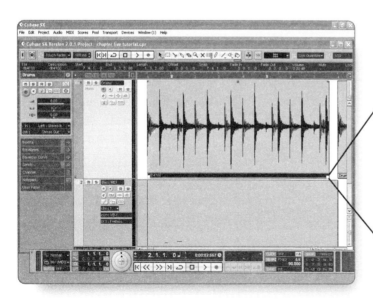

Resizing MIDI Parts

With the four-bar drum part in place starting at bar 10, we are now going copy the bass over to play along; however, we are going to make some edits to the bass and give it a slight variation.

NOTE

Zooming Shortcut

You will need to use the Shift + F key command to zoom out over the project for the following steps.

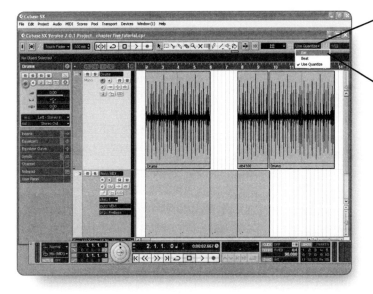

1. **Click** on the **Grid Type menu.** The Grid Type menu will appear.

2. **Click** on **Bar.** The grid will now be set to snap to a bar.

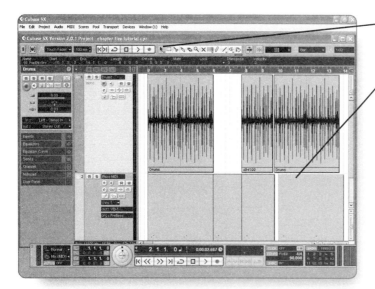

3. **Click** on the **Selection tool**. The pointer will become an arrow.

4. **Alt + Click** (Windows)/ **Command + Click** (Macintosh) on the **four-bar bass part** that starts on bar 2, and drag it to bar 10. The bass part will be copied to bar 10.

Now let's alter the bass part.

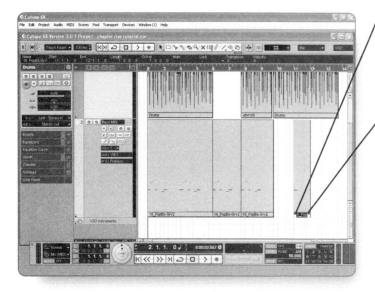

5. **Click** on the **left handle** of the bass part starting on bar 10, and **drag** it to bar 11 (the grid will automatically snap to bar 11).

6. **Click** on the **right handle** and **drag** it to bar 12. The end of the bass part will resize to end on bar 12.

6

Audio Editing— Sample Editor and Audio Part Editor

In Chapter 5 we looked at how to work with audio events (as well as MIDI parts) in the project window to build the arrangement of your project. In this chapter we will learn to edit audio events. We'll look at the Audio Sample Editor (or Sample Editor); this editor is used when you want to clean up your recordings or make Regions from the recordings that you can quickly add to the various points in the project. We'll also work with the Audio Part Editor. Audio parts consist of multiple audio events that are grouped together to provide you with an easy way to arrange your project in the project window.

In this chapter, you'll learn how to:

- ⬤ Edit audio events in the Sample Editor
- ⬤ Create and use Regions
- ⬤ Work with overlapping audio events and crossfades
- ⬤ Edit audio parts in the Audio Part Editor
- ⬤ Create and work hit points

Editing Audio Events

There are two types of audio content that can be placed on an audio track: an audio event and an audio part. What's the difference? An audio event is simply an audio recording that starts at the point in the project where you began recording, or the position at which you imported an audio file (more on importing audio in Chapter 15). An audio part, on the other hand, allows you to group multiple audio events together, making it easier to arrange multiple events as one (more on audio parts later in this chapter).

Loading the Tutorial Project

We'll begin with opening the tutorial project for this chapter (tutorial projects can be downloaded from **www.courseptr. com/downloads**).

> ### NOTE
>
> **One Project at a Time**
>
> Although Cubase can open several projects at one time, it is recommended that you close any open projects before continuing.

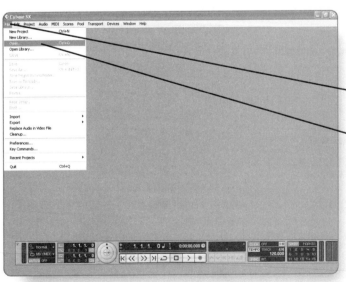

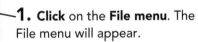

1. Click on the **File menu**. The File menu will appear.

2. Click on **Open**. The Open Project dialog will appear.

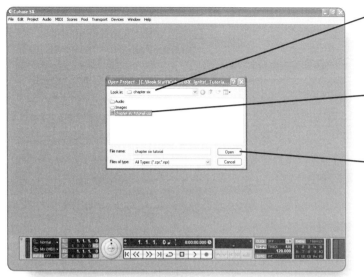

3. Navigate to the **location** on your computer where you extracted the Chapter 6.zip tutorial.

4. Click on **chapter six tutorial.cpr**. The project will become highlighted.

5. Click on **Open**. The project will be loaded.

NOTE

CPR Extension

For Windows users, the file extension .cpr may not appear in the Open Project dialog window, depending on your settings.

Trimming the Audio Event

The project consists of a single track of drums, with an audio event starting at bar 3. The audio event is just under 4 bars long; the first two bars are a simple drum beat, and a drum fill starts at bar 5. We are going to open this drum audio event in the Sample Editor. In the Editor, we'll learn to set the start and end points of the audio event (sometimes referred to as trimming the event). We'll also learn to create Regions from the event, which can be placed easily at any point of the song, again allowing you to build an entire arrangement with ease.

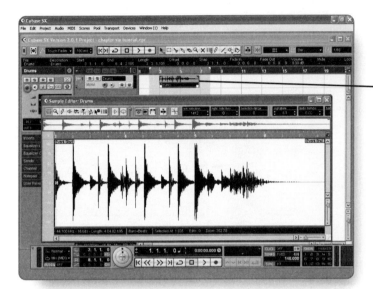

Let's begin by opening the drum track in the audio into the Sample Editor.

1. Double-click on the **audio event** on the drums track. The Audio Event Editor will appear with the drum recording loaded.

NOTE

Launching the Sample Window

The sample window will open if you double-click on an audio event from the project window; double-clicking on an audio part will open the Part Editor (more on audio parts and the Part Editor later in this chapter).

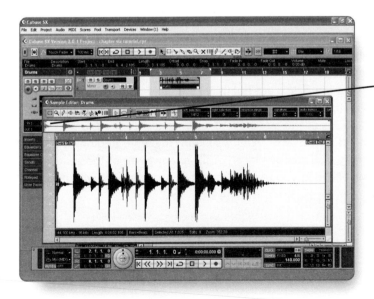

Now you will need to zoom into the beginning portion of the drum sample.

2. On the upper half of the sample overview window, **click and drag** around the **first drum hit** of the sample. A blue box will be drawn around the hit. The sample window will zoom around the first drum hit.

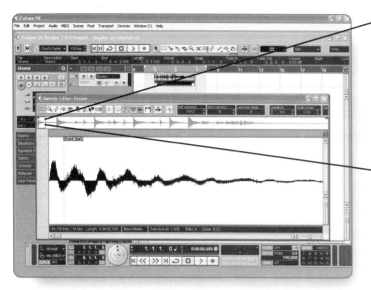

3. **Place** the **mouse pointer** on the lower half of the sample overview window within the blue box that surrounds the first drum hit. The mouse cursor will become a Hand tool. The Hand tool will allow you to move the blue box.

4. **Click and drag** the **blue box** all the way to the left, so that the sample window displays the very beginning of the event.

NOTE

The Blue Box

When using the sample overview window to zoom to certain points of the event, think of the blue box as a window of what you'll see in the Sample Editor. This window can be moved (by using the Hand tool as described earlier), enlarged, or shrunk by clicking and dragging on the right or left part of the box. You can also draw around the portion of the sample you want to zoom in on by clicking and dragging on the upper portion of the overview window (also described earlier).

TIP

Using the Rule to Zoom

You can also zoom in and out of the Sample Editor by clicking on the ruler above the editor window and dragging down to zoom in, and dragging up to zoom out.

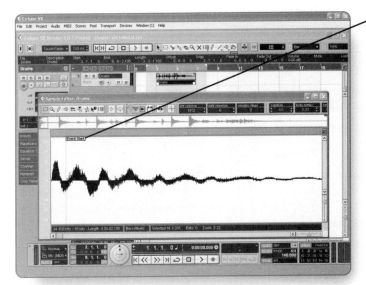

5. Click on the **Event Start marker** in the Sample Editor and drag it to just before the drum hit starts. Now the event will start playing at the point where the drum starts, eliminating any silence at the beginning.

In the project window, the drum event did start at bar 3; however, because we trimmed the beginning of the event, the start time will now be a little later. So we are going to need to go back to the project window to fix this.

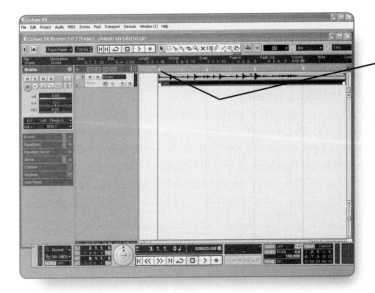

Begin by zooming into the beginning of the event.

1. Click and drag downward on the bottom half of the project window ruler on bar 3. The project window will zoom into bar 3, which is where the event starts. You'll want to zoom in quite a bit to see the gap between bar 3 and the start of the event.

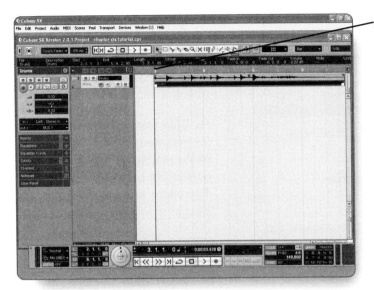

2. Click and drag the **event** to bar 3. Because the grid is set to Bar, the event should snap to bar 3 when you attempt to move it.

CAUTION

**Zoom Out
Before Playback**

Before you begin playback, it would be a good idea to zoom out on the project window so you can see the project cursor play over the entire event.

Creating Regions

Regions allow you to capture a portion of an audio event and place it on the event's Region list. From this list you can later pull Regions out and place them at any point in the project window. This allows you to use these Regions like building blocks to arrange a track in the project window. We are going to demonstrate this by creating two Regions; one will be the main beat of the drum sample, and the other will be the fill.

We'll begin by capturing the main beat portion of the drum sample.

1. Double-click on the **drum audio event** from the project window. The Sample Editor will open.

2. Press Shift + F to zoom the Sample Editor out to full.

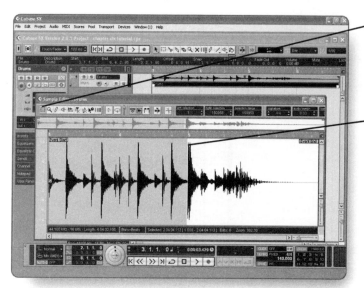

3. By default, the Range Selection tool should be the selected tool; if it isn't, **click** on the **Range Selection tool** on the toolbar.

4. Click just before the **drum hit** that starts on bar 5 and drag all the way to the left. The first 4 bars will become highlighted. These four bars are the main beat of the drum sample.

TIP

Tool Selection Shortcut

As with the project window, you can also select tools by right-clicking (Control + Click for one button Macintosh users) in the Sample Editor and selecting the tool from the pop-up menu.

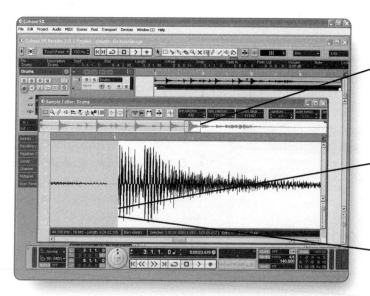

Now you will need to fine trim the selected range.

5. Click on the **upper half of the overview window** and **drag** with your mouse **around the drum hit** on bar 5. The Sample Editor will zoom in around this hit.

6. Place your **mouse pointer** over the edge of the selected range. The mouse will become a double-sided arrow.

7. Click and drag the **selection** so that it ends just before the drum hit on bar 5.

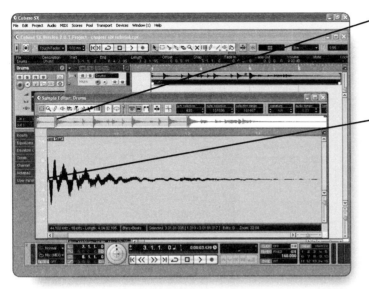

8. Click and drag on the **upper half of the overview window** around the first hit of the sample. The Sample Editor will zoom to the first hit.

9. Place your **mouse pointer** over the range edge (which should be at the start point of the sample) and **drag** to the **right** so that the range starts where the drum hit occurs.

NOTE

Starting Point Reference

In a previous exercise, we moved the event start to just in front of the first drum hit; you can use this point as your reference for where you should drag the range start to. It is possible for a range to overlap the start and end points of an audio event. If the range selection goes beyond these points, the range selection will be a darker shade of blue, indicating that the range is outside the event area.

TIP

Zoom Out Shortcut

After setting the Region's start and end points, it's a good idea to fully zoom out so that you can see the entire sample in the Editor. You can do this by pressing Shift + F (both Windows and Macintosh).

Now visually you have the correct range selected; however, the best judge of this will be your ears. We will now look at how you can audition the range in Loop mode to ensure that the selected range sounds just right.

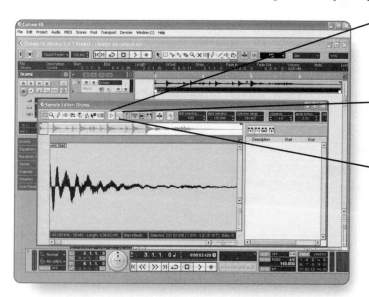

10. Click on the **Audition Loop button**. This will make the audition playback automatically loop the range.

11. Click on the **Audition button**. The range will begin playback.

12. Click on the **Audition button** again to end the preview.

TIP

Adjusting Volume

You can control the volume of the sample audition by adjusting the slider just to the right of the Audition Loop button.

Now with the range set, we'll create a Region.

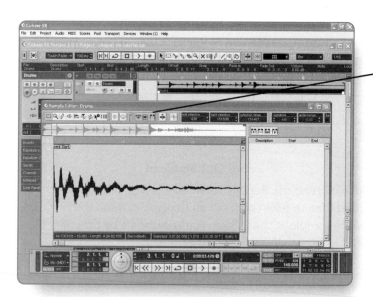

- The Show Regions button may already be inactive; items such as this are part of SX's layout preferences, and are not saved with the project. Therefore, if you have opened the Regions view prior to opening this project, the Regions window will already be opened; if it is not, then click on the Show Regions button. The Regions list will appear on the right side of the Sample Editor window.

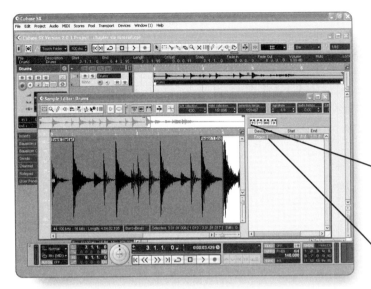

1. Click on the **Add Region button**. The Region will be added to the list and the name will become highlighted.

2. Type in the name '**Main Beat**' and **press Enter**. The Region will be named.

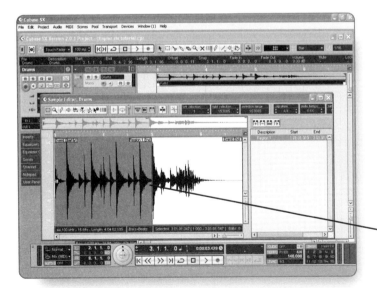

You now have one Region of the main beat of the drums. Next we are going to create a second Region, and this one will be the drum fill.

Start by selecting the drum fill portion of the sample.

1. Press Shift + F to zoom out full on the Sample Editor window.

2. Click just in front of the **drum hit** that starts at bar 5 and drag all the way to the right. The section of the sample containing the drum fill will be selected.

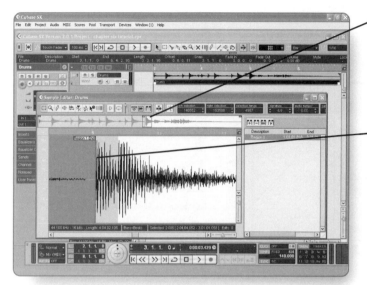

3. Click on the upper half of the **overview window** at the first hit of the drum fill on bar 5, and **drag** the **pointer** around the hit. The Sample Editor will zoom to the first hit of the drum fill.

4. Place the **mouse pointer** over the edge of the range selection. The pointer will become a double-sided arrow.

5. Click and drag the selected **range** so that it starts just before the first hit of the drum loop.

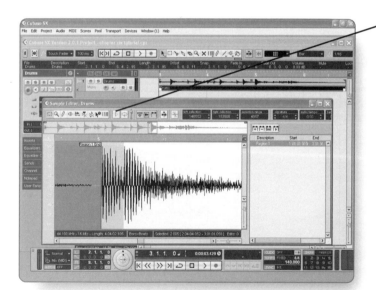

6. Click on the **Audition button**. The range will begin to play in Loop mode. Listen and check that the start point of the range point is correct. The first hit shouldn't sound cut off or begin too early.

NOTE

Loop Audition

The loop audition should still be active after the previous exercise; if it's not, you will need to click on the Loop Audition button prior to auditioning the range.

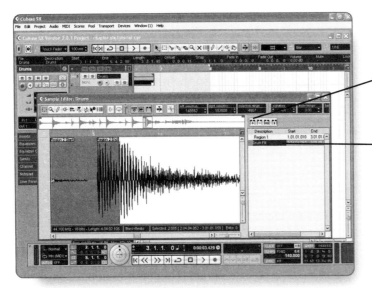

Once the range selection sounds just right, we'll make a Region for the drum fill.

7. **Click** on the **Add Region button**. A new Region will be created and become highlighted.

8. **Type** in '**Drum Fill**' and **press Enter**. The Region will be named.

TIP

Using the Play Region Button

You can audition a Region by selecting it from the list and clicking the Play Region button above the Region list.

You will now have two Regions in the Regions list: main beat and drum fill. Next we are going to look at how we can use these Regions to build your arrangements. To demonstrate this, we are going to arrange a 4-bar drum beat that ends with a drum fill.

1. **Click** under the first **column** of the Main Beat Region (it will be called Region 1 if you didn't rename it) and drag it to bar 7 on the drum track in the project window. The Region containing the drum beat will be inserted into the track.

CAUTION

Dragging Regions Warning

When dragging the Region to the project window, you must be careful to drag it to the correct track. If you mistakenly drag the Region to an area where no track exists, a new track will automatically be created, and the Region will be placed on that track.

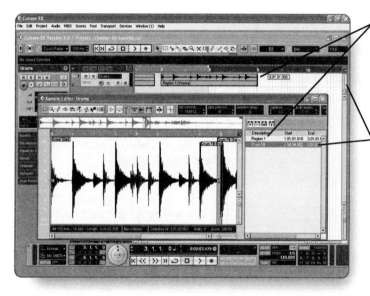

2. **Click** on the **first column** of the Main Beat Region (it will be called Region 1 if you didn't rename it) and drag it to bar 9 of the drum track. The Region will be placed on the track.

3. **Click** on the **first column** of the Drum Fill Region and drag it to bar 11 of the drum track. The Region will be placed on the track.

Now the drum track will have a 4-bar beat starting on bar 7, ending with a fill that starts on bar 11. Using Regions, it is very easy to build an entire arrangement in minutes.

Working with Overlapping Audio Events and Creating Crossfades

When arranging audio events in the project window, there may be times when an audio event might overlap another; however, a track can play only one audio event at a time. Whichever audio event is set "to the Front" will be played at the point the overlapping events occur. It is possible to have the track play both events; this is done by using crossfades. A crossfade creates and inserts a new audio event of the overlapping section. This new file event contains both events—one will be fading out while the other fades in. You can also edit the fade out and fade in times.

Setting an Audio Event to the Front

As mentioned, when two events are overlapping each other, only the event that is set to the front will be played. To demonstrate how to set an event "to Front" we'll need to create an overlap of audio events.

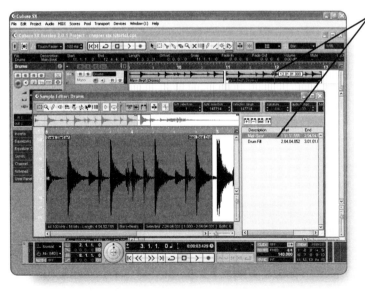

1. **Insert** an **instance** of the Main Beat Region to bar 12. The Region will be placed on the track at bar 12. The Region will overlap with the tail portion of the drum fill that starts on bar 11; the overlapping section is indicated by a darker shade of gray.

By default, the new Region will be set as the "to Front" event, meaning that when the project cursor reaches bar 12, the drum fill will stop playing and the Main Beat Region will start. We are going to change this so that the drum fill plays until the end, at which point the main beat will begin.

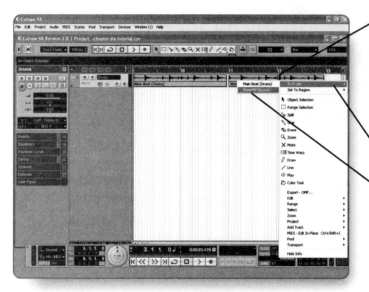

2. Right-click (Command + Click for Macintosh users) on the **Main Beat range** from the project window. The project window's pop-up menu will appear.

3. Click on **To Front**. The To Front submenu will appear.

4. Click on **Drum Fill (Drums)**. Now the drum fill will be set to play over the top of the main beat that starts on bar 12.

To change the front event back to the Main Beat Region, do the following:

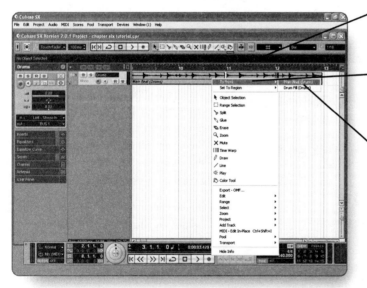

5. Right-click (Command + Click for Macintosh users) on the Drum Fill Region.

6. Click on **To Front** from the pop-up menu. The To Front submenu will appear.

7. Click on **Main Beat** from the submenu. The main beat will be restored to play over the drum fill.

Creating and Editing Crossfades

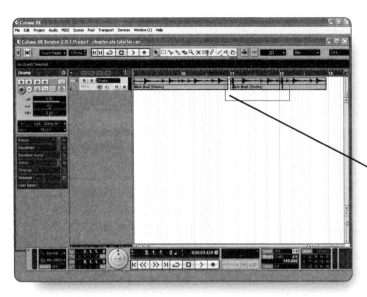

It is also possible to have both parts of an overlap play. This is done by creating a crossfade. A crossfade will create a fade out on the first overlapping event and a fade in on the second. Let's begin by creating the crossfade.

1. **Click and drag** your **mouse** around the drum fill that starts at bar 11 and the Main Beat Region starting at bar 12. Both events will be selected.

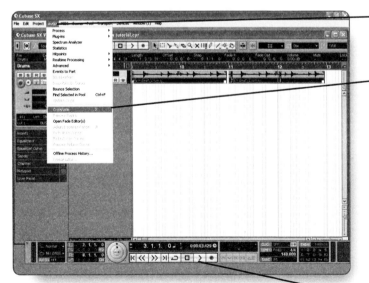

2. **Click** on the **Audio menu**. The Audio drop-down menu will appear.

3. **Click** on **Crossfade**. A crossfade will be created on the overlapping portion of the two events.

TIP

A crossfade can also be created by pressing the X key on both Windows and Macintosh platforms.

---

4. **Play back** the **project**. You will hear the crossfade as you play the piece.

> **TIP**
>
> **Playback from Cursor**
>
> You don't have to listen to the entire project when you only want to hear the changes you made on bar 12; simply click on the ruler above the project window at bar 11 and the project cursor will be moved to bar 11. When the Play button is clicked, playback will begin from the cursor position.

The first thing you may think when listening to the crossfade is that the fade length is too long, creating a gap, volume-wise, in the track. To fix this, we'll need to edit the crossfade.

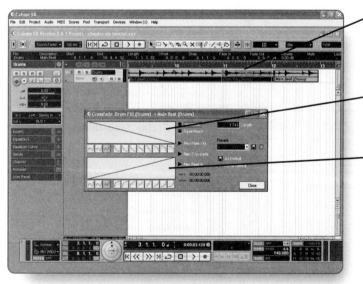

1. Double-click on the **dark gray area** that contains the crossfade. The Crossfade Editor will appear.

- The top Fade Editor window displays the fade out of the first overlapping events.

- The bottom Fade Editor window displays the fade in for the second overlapping event.

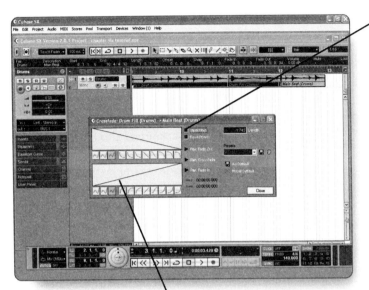

2. Click on the **Equal Gain button** to uncheck this option.

> **NOTE**
>
> **Equal Gain**
>
> When the Equal Gain option is checked, if any changes are made to either Fade Editor, the other Editor will automatically change to match.

For this crossfade, we want to have the second event's fade short so that the drums have no drastic volume changes. The fade out of the first event can be left the way it is, as it is the ringing tones of the drummer's toms.

3. Click on the **fade line** of the bottom Fade Editor. A black dot will be placed on the line. This dot represents a changing point of the fade.

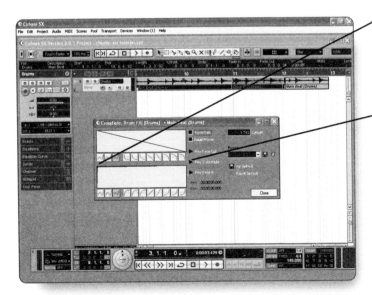

4. Click and drag the black **dot** to the top-left corner of the Fade Editor.

Now audition the crossfade.

5. Click on the **Play Crossfade button**. The crossfade will begin playback. Check that the fade in on the second event (Bottom Editor) isn't too long, creating an uneven volume change to the drum track.

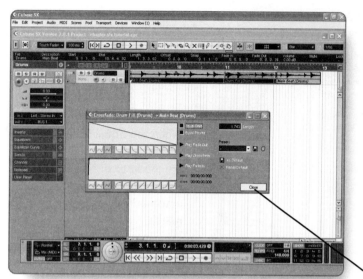

TIP

Previewing Individual Fades

It is also possible to listen to the individual fades by clicking on the Play Fade Out button to play the top fade edit and the Play Fade In button to play the bottom fade edit.

Now apply the changes.

6. **Click** on **Close**. The changes will be applied to the crossfade.

The Audio Part Editor

Now we are going to move on to working with audio parts. An audio part is essentially multiple audio events or Regions grouped together. Grouping events or Regions will help you when building the arrangement of your project. Let's say you have a drum track in which the parts of the first verse are the same as the second verse. You could simply arrange the various events to build the first verse, group them as an audio part, and then copy it to the second verse.

Creating an Audio Part

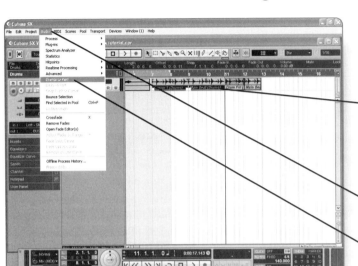

We'll begin by creating an audio part from the last few Regions that we added to the project, including the crossfade portion.

1. Click and drag your **mouse pointer** around the area that you would like to create a part from. The Regions will become highlighted.

2. Click on the **Audio menu**. The Audio submenu will appear.

3. Click on **Events to Part**. All the Regions will be grouped together into one audio part.

Editing an Audio Part

Now we are going to take a look at how you can edit the events that are contained in an audio part.

1. Double-click on the **audio part**. The Audio Part Editor will appear.

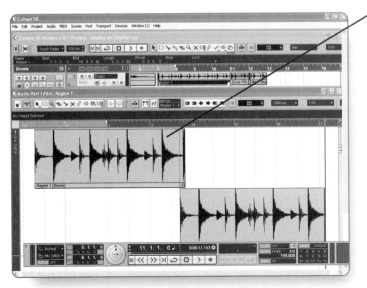

NOTE

Zoom In to View Events

When the editor opens, it may or may not be zoomed out full depending on the last layout used of the Audio Part Editor; if it is, you will have to zoom in so you can see the events better.

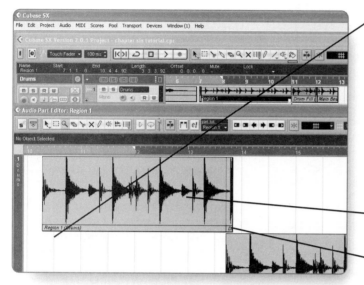

• The Audio Part Editor has several "lanes" that are used when editing the events with this part. This makes it easier for you to get a clear picture of what you are editing when working with events in a part that overlaps.

Let's take a look at how to resize an event.

2. Click on any **event**. The event will become selected.

3. Click and drag the event's ending **handle** to the left ; the handle should snap to the bars as you drag.

Now let's apply a fade in to the start of the audio part.

4. Click on the first **event** in the audio part. The event will become highlighted.

5. Click on the small blue **triangle** in the top-left corner of the event and **drag** it inwards. The event will now display a fade in at the beginning of the event.

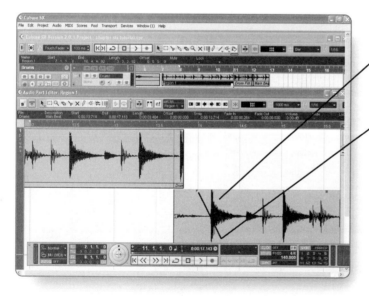

NOTE

Alternative Fade Out Method

You can also apply fade outs to events by clicking and dragging the blue triangle on the top-right corner of the event to the left.

TIP

Removing Clicks and Pops

When placing two events directly next to each other, the difference in volume between the end of one event and the start of another can create small clicks or pops in the part. Applying small fade ins and fade outs can help smooth out the transition.

Next we'll change the volume of an individual event in an audio part.

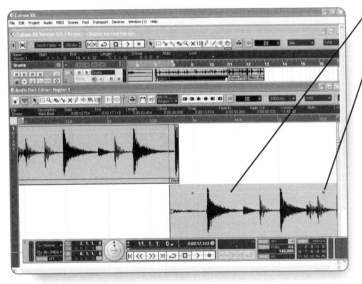

6. **Click** on any **event**. The event will become selected.

7. **Click and drag** the **blue square** downward. This decreases the volume of this event. The display will reflect the changes.

NOTE

Automatic Crossfade Edit

When adjusting the volume of an event that includes a crossfade, such as the one in this exercise, the crossfade will automatically be edited to reflect the changes made to the event's volume.

NOTE

Copies Are Not Affected

Changing the volume, applying fades, or even resizing events is applied individually to each event in the audio part; if there are copies of the event elsewhere in the part, these events will not be affected.

Auditioning Events in an Audio Part

Just like the Sample Editor we looked at earlier, the Audio Part Editor also allows you to audition a selected event in the audio part.

1. **Click** on the **event** you want to audition. The event will become selected.

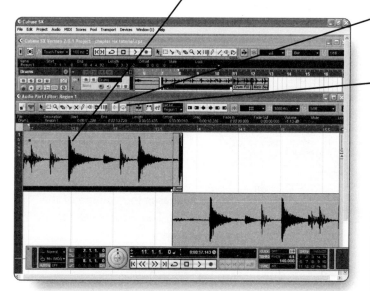

2. **Click** on the **Audition button**. Playback of the event will begin.

3. **Click** on the **Audition Loop button**. The event's audition will loop.

NOTE

Automatic Loop Audition

If you want to use loop audition, you only need to click the Loop Audition button after selecting the event; the audition will automatically begin.

NOTE

Using Tools in the Audio Part Editor

All the tools that we looked at in Chapter 5, such as the Eraser, Split, and Glue tools, work in the same manner in the Audio Part Editor. Refer to Chapter 5 for more on how to use these tools.

7

Editing MIDI

In Chapter 4, we looked at recording MIDI, and just as with audio, MIDI can be edited to perfect your recordings. One of the attractive things about working with MIDI is how you can edit the performance with precision; in an audio recording, if a note is played out of tune, or played with less than perfect timing, the only practical option is to go back and record it again. With MIDI, however, it is possible to edit the odd misplayed note or tighten up some sloppy timing. This is perfect for musicians who, like me, find keyboard playing a challenge.

In this chapter, you'll learn how to:

● Edit MIDI note information

● Fix poor timing with Quantize

Editing MIDI Note Information

Working in MIDI is just like writing a letter in a word processor. Every time you strike a key, a letter appears on the screen; this letter can then be altered to suit your tastes. You can change the color, size, or even the font. When you create MIDI data, you play a key on your MIDI keyboard and the note appears in Cubase. These notes can later be altered to suit the style of the song, or just to fix up some mistakes made during the recording. You can edit the note's length, the note's velocity (velocity represents how loud or how much force was used to play the note), and more. We are going to take a look at some of the common ways to edit MIDI.

The Tutorial Project

By this point you know how to load projects into SX. For this chapter you will need to open the Chapter 7 tutorial project, which you should have downloaded from the book's companion site. If you're unsure how to open a project, refer to Chapter 5 for more on loading projects (be sure to choose the correct project for this chapter). If you don't have access to the tutorial, you should record a four-bar MIDI event.

The project will contain a single MIDI track containing a four-bar synthesizer bass line. The project is already set up so that the MIDI track plays the A1 VST instrument (we'll take a closer look at VST instruments in Chapter 8).

Changing Pitch

Let's start by changing a note's pitch. In the bass MIDI part, there are a few notes that were not played correctly when the part was recorded. We are going to fix these notes.

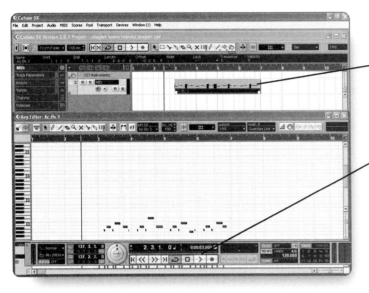

Begin by opening the MIDI Key Editor.

1. **Double-click** on the **bass MIDI part**. The Key Editor will open. You may need to zoom in to get a better view of the individual notes.

2. **Click** on the **Play button**. Playback will begin.

NOTE

Live Editing

This project has been set so that the MIDI part will play in a continuous loop. With SX it is possible to edit MIDI information while playing back; this can be helpful when performing edits so that you can hear the effects of your changes almost instantly.

While listening to the bass loop, your ears may tell you that the pitch of a few notes seems wrong—one in bar 4 and one in bar 5. These are the notes we need to fix.

3. **Click** on the **D#2 note** on bar 4, beat 3. Clicking on the note will trigger the playback of that note. The note will also become highlighted (selected).

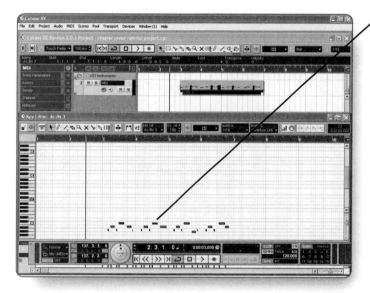

4. **Drag** the **note** down to C2. The C note will now play when the project cursor reaches it.

> ## NOTE
> ### Scrubbing
> While dragging the note, you will trigger the play-back of every note you pass until you reach C2. This is helpful in making sure you're dragging the note to the correct pitch.

> ## TIP
> ### Using the Keyboard as a Guide
> When you are moving notes in the Key Editor, use the keyboard on the left as your guide. Keys will be highlighted to indicate the current position of your mouse pointer.

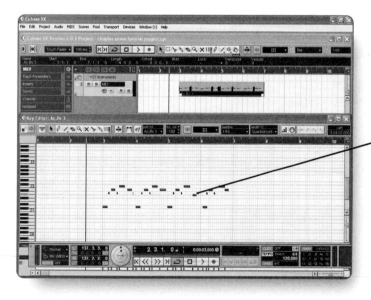

Now let's change the incorrect note in bar 5.

5. **Click** on the **G#1 note** in bar 5, beat 4 and **drag** it **up** to B1. The note will become a B note.

Now the bass part will sound better with no notes being played out of tune.

Changing Note Length

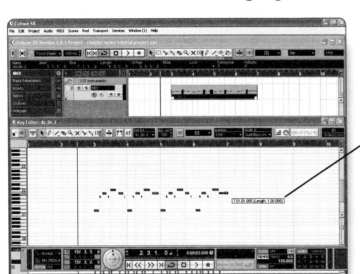

Sometimes when recording, you may release the key of your MIDI controller too quickly, or you might hold the key too long. The note's length can also be adjusted.

1. **Place** your **mouse pointer** over the right edge of the last note in the bass part. The pointer will become a double-sided arrow.

2. **Click and drag** the **note** to bar 7. The note's length will extend to the end of bar 6.

NOTE

Changing Starting Time

By clicking and dragging on the right side of the note, you can extend the note's length. You can also click and drag on the left side of the note; however, this will change the starting point of the note, not just the note's length. If you want to adjust only the length, in most cases you should click and drag on the right side of the note.

Changing a Note's Timing

It frequently happens that when recording MIDI, many keyboard players will play a few notes either a touch too early or a tad too late. Thanks to MIDI's editing capabilities, these few notes can be quickly corrected.

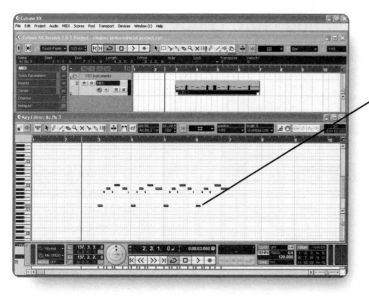

In our tutorial project there are a few notes on bar 6 that were played late. Let's correct these notes.

1. **Click** on the **first note** of bar 6 and drag it to the left so that it lines up to the first beat of bar 6. The note will now be played with correct timing.

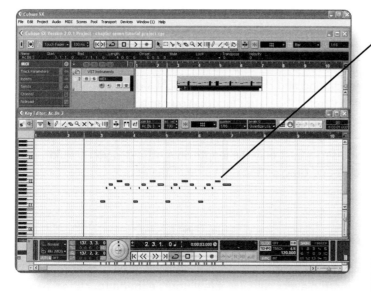

Now correct the note on beat 3.

2. **Click** on the **note** that is just to the right of beat 3 of bar 6 and **drag** it to the **left** so that it lines up with beat 3.

NOTE

Notes Snap To Grid

When moving notes in the Key Editor, the notes will also snap to a grid so that they start at correct timing positions. The grid size is set by the Quantize menu on the top of the Key Edit window. By default, it is set to 16th-note resolution.

Changing Velocities

In simple terms, velocity is the volume of a note; the harder you strike a note on your MIDI keyboard, the louder the note will play. Sometimes when recording you may hit a few notes too hard or too soft; again, there is no need to re-record the part, because you can quickly edit the notes' velocity.

With our tutorial project, there are a few notes that were played with inconsistent velocity. We'll need to change these notes.

1. **Click** on the **Show Info button** if it is not already high-lighted. The information lane will appear above the Key Editor window.

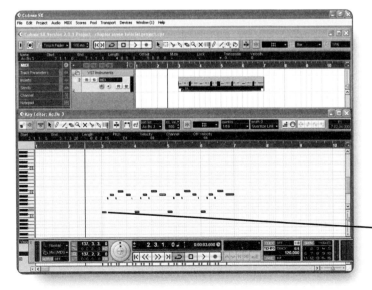

NOTE

The Show Info Button

The Show Info button may not be active. If it is active, you can continue to step 2. The Show Info setting is saved independently of the project settings. This means that if you open the information lane and do not close it before exiting SX, it will be open the next time you start or open a new project.

2. **Click** on the **note** at beat 1 of bar 3. The note will become selected.

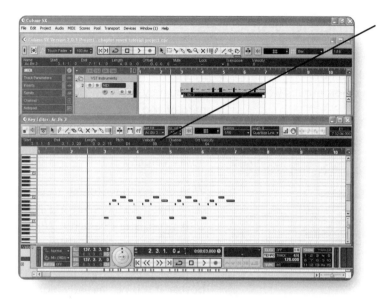

- Velocity is measured with a numerical value between 0 and 127, with 0 being the softest and 127 the hardest. When making changes to velocity it's a good idea to know the velocity of the surrounding notes. Then you know what range the velocity should be changed to so that the velocities remain consistent. Here we can see that the first note's velocity is 89; a range of 85-90 will make the velocities sound smooth with no sudden volume changes.

3. Click on the **note** at beat 3 of bar 3. The note will become selected. This note was played too softly, so we'll need to raise its velocity.

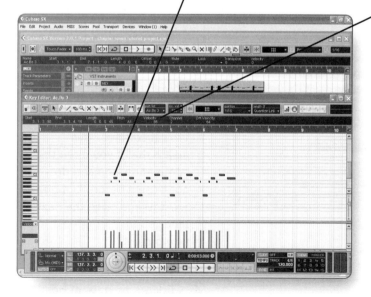

4. Click on the **velocity amount** from the information lane in the Key Editor window. The velocity amount will become highlighted.

5. Type in **86** and **press Enter.** The note velocity will now be 86.

> **NOTE**
>
> **Velocity Values**
>
> Remember that a value between 85 and 90 should keep your velocities consistent. However, this is not written in stone. Feel free to experiment with these values. If you have a song in which you want to have a sudden change in velocity, you can try different values that are much higher or lower.

Next we need to lower the velocity of a different note.

6. Click on the **note** at beat 4 of bar 4. The note will become selected.

7. Click on the **velocity amount** from the information lane. The amount will become highlighted.

8. Type in **85** and **press Enter.** The note velocity is now 85.

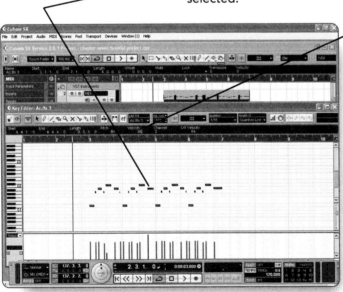

> **TIP**
>
> **Note Colors**
>
> You may have noticed that the notes in the Key editor are color coded; the color of the note represents its velocity amount. A darker color represents softer velocities, whereas brighter colors represent higher velocities.

What if you have a recording in which the velocities vary greatly throughout the part? I am sure you would not want to manually change the value of each note. In addition, there may be a situation in which you will want all the velocities to be in a specific range. Let's take a look at how you can change the velocity of several notes at once.

Start by selecting all the notes in the part.

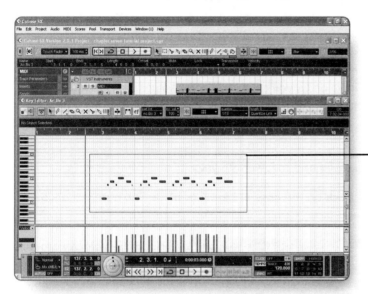

1. **Click and drag** your **mouse pointer** around all the notes. As you drag a black rectangle will appear indicating the area that will be selected when you release your mouse. The notes will become selected.

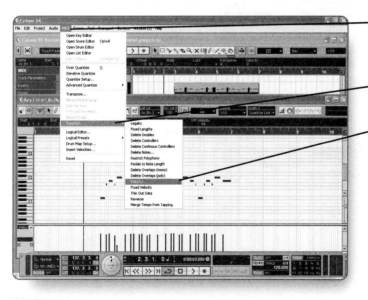

2. **Click** on the **MIDI menu**. The MIDI drop-down menu will appear.

3. **Click** on **Functions**. The Functions submenu will appear.

4. **Click** on **Velocity**. The Velocity dialog window will appear.

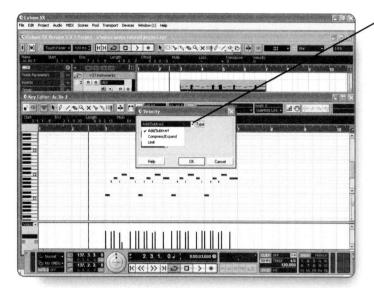

5. **Click** on the **Type menu**. The Type pop-up menu will appear.

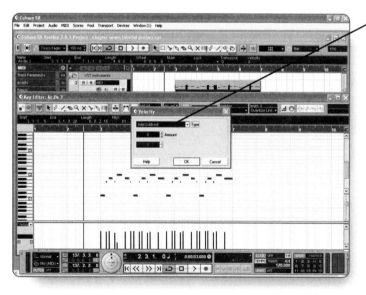

● **Add/Subtract**. This type will add or subtract to the existing note velocity. For example, if you enter a value of 5 in the Amount field, the velocity of all selected notes will be increased by a value of 5. Enter a negative value to decrease the velocity values.

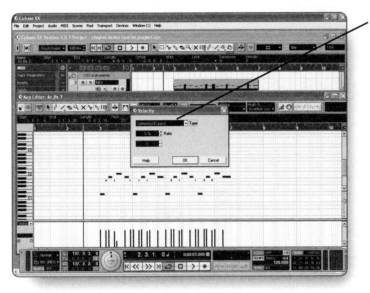

- **Compress/Expand**. This type might be a little confusing if you are new to Cubase or MIDI. Compress/Expand attempts to control the velocities much like a hardware compressor/expander would. It evens out the velocities by reducing (compressing) those that go over certain levels. A reverse effect can be applied that will create drastic changes in the velocities (Expand). Entering a value of 100% or lower in the Ratio field will compress the velocities; a Ratio value above 100% (with a maximum of 300%) will begin to expand the velocities.

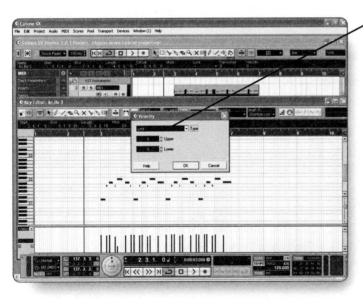

- **Limit**. This type will allow you to restrict a note's velocity to a certain range. The velocity will not go over the value entered in the Upper field. In addition, the velocity will not go below the value entered in the Lower field. This type is helpful when you want to place several notes with varying velocities in a determined range, making the velocities more consistent.

Let's demonstrate applying velocities to multiple notes. We will place all the notes' velocities into a narrow value range of 87-90. For this we'll use the Limit velocity type.

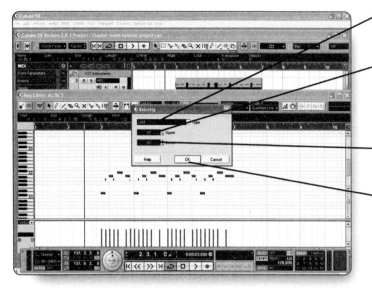

6. Click on **Limit** from the Type drop-down menu.

7. Click in the **Upper field**. The default value of 0 will become highlighted. **Type** in **90** and **press Enter**.

8. Click in the **Lower field**. **Type** in **87** and **press Enter**.

9. Click on **OK**. The changes will be applied to the selected notes.

NOTE

Observing Velocity Changes

The velocity changes are very slight and might be hard to hear. You can see the changes by selecting the individual notes from the Key editor and reading the values in the Velocity field.

Quantizing MIDI

Earlier we learned to fix the timing on individual notes that may have been played badly. But what if the part you recorded has several notes that need their timing fixed? It could be tedious to fix each note individually. For a situation like this, you'll want to use the Quantize function. Quantize will automatically move notes to an exact time position. By setting the Quantize value to an eighth note and applying it, all the notes will automatically move so that they are placed accurately on an eighth note position.

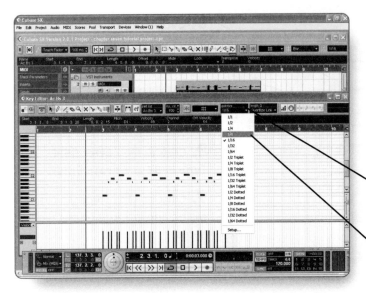

To demonstrate how to use Quantize, we are going to change the MIDI part in our tutorial project so that all the notes are moved to be played at eighth notes only.

Begin by setting the Quantize value to an eighth note.

1. Click on the **Quantize menu**. The Quantize drop-down menu will appear.

2. Click on **1-8 Note**. The Quantize value will change to an eighth note.

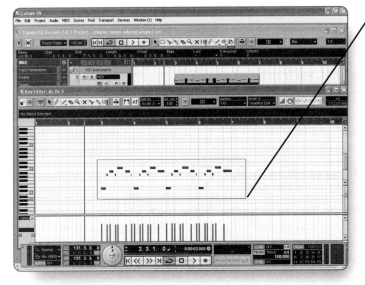

3. Click and drag the **mouse pointer** around all the notes in the Key editor. As you drag a rectangle will appear indicating the area that will be selected. The notes will become selected.

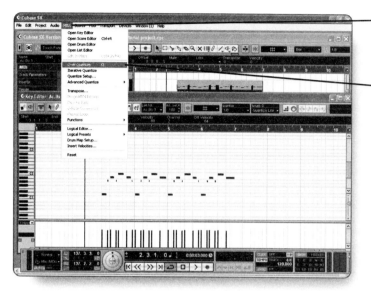

4. Click on the **MIDI menu**. The MIDI drop-down menu will appear.

5. Click on **Over Quantize**. The notes will automatically snap to eighth note positions.

NOTE

Quantizing Other Time Divisions

In this exercise we Quantized all the notes so that they start on eighth notes. You can also Quantize the notes to other time divisions, such as 16th notes or 32nd notes, by choosing a different setting in step 2 of the preceding exercise. The setting you use depends on how much timing correction is needed and the style of music you are working with.

TIP

Quantization Shortcut

You can also apply Quantization by pressing "Q" on your computer's keyboard when the desired notes are selected.

8

Working with VST Instruments

When Cubase was first released, it was primarily a MIDI sequencer—a way to record and edit performances from MIDI-equipped devices such as synthesizers and drum machines. In the years that followed, Cubase began focusing on adding support for recording and editing audio. In 1998, with the release of Cubase VST 3.7, Steinberg took these two worlds to the next level, resulting in *VST instruments*. These instruments work in the same manner as traditional synthesizers and drum machines; however, your computer is the device creating the sounds, and the outputs of the instruments are connected internally to the Cubase Mixer, allowing you to mix them in your project as you do with audio tracks.

In this chapter, you'll learn how to:

- Load a VST instrument to a project
- Assign a MIDI track to a VST instrument
- Conserve your CPU by freezing a VST instrument

Loading a VST Instrument

Before you can do anything with VST instruments, you will need to load one into your project, much like turning on and connecting a traditional synthesizer.

NOTE

Tutorial

As with the last few chapters, there is a tutorial project to be used with the following exercises. Before continuing, you need to open the Chapter 8 tutorial project. The project will contain one MIDI track with a small MIDI part that will be used to play the VST instrument that we'll load later in this chapter.

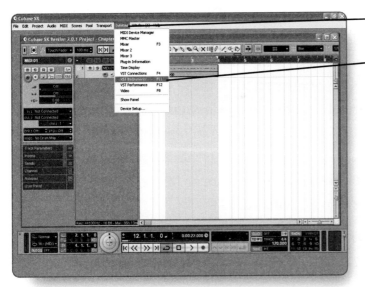

1. Click on the **Devices menu**. The Devices menu will appear.

2. Click on **VST Instruments**. The VST Instrument rack window will appear.

TIP

VST Shortcut

You can also open the VST Instrument rack window by pressing F11 (Windows and Macintosh).

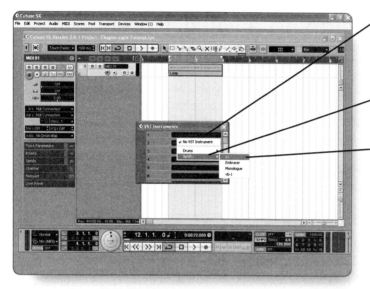

3. Click on the **first instrument rack slot**. A pop-up menu of available VST instruments will appear.

4. Click on **Synths**. The Synth submenu will appear.

5. Click on **a1**. The instrument will be added to the slot and will appear on your screen.

6. Close the **a1 window**. The project window will come to the front.

That's really all there is to it. Every VST instrument will have a different number of audio and MIDI connections; this information is automatically passed to SX by the instrument.

The purpose of this chapter is to familiarize you with loading VST instruments and assigning a MIDI track to play the instruments. We won't be covering the details of a1 synth; if you want to learn more about this instrument, consult SX's documentation.

NOTE

Third-party VSTs

You're not limited to working with just those VST instruments that come with Cubase SX. You can purchase third-party VST instruments from vendors such as Native Instruments, IK Multimedia, and even Steinberg. When you become comfortable working with VST instruments, I recommend having a look at some of these.

Assigning a MIDI Track to an Instrument

Now that you have the VST instrument loaded, all the MIDI ports that can be connected to it have been added to SX's list of available ports. Before a MIDI track can play an instrument, you need to connect the output of the track to the instrument.

1. Click on **Show Inspector**. The MIDI channel's properties will open.

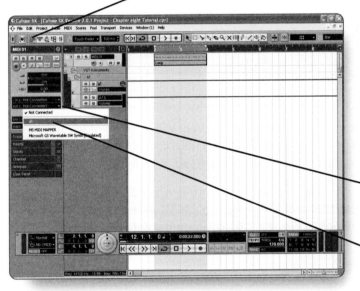

NOTE

The Inspector

Depending on your current settings, the Inspector may already be open. If so, continue to step 2.

2. Click on the MIDI track's **Output menu**. The Output drop-down menu will appear.

3. Click on **a1**. The track's output is now connected to the a1 instrument.

NOTE

MIDI Tracks

If you are working with a project that contains several MIDI tracks, you will need to select the correct MIDI track from the project window before assigning the output to a VST instrument.

NOTE

MIDI Channels

MIDI devices such as hardware synthesizers typically are equipped with 16 channels; this allows you to have 16 different MIDI tracks play the device (for example, one track might play a piano sound, while another track plays a string sound). Some VST instruments may not have multiple channels (check the documentation of any third-party instruments for channel availability). The a1 synth is equipped with only one MIDI channel, meaning that the a1 can play only one sound at a time. If you want to have the a1 play several sounds, you will need to load more than one instance of the instrument. For more on working with several MIDI channels, consult SX's documentation or Robert Guerin's *Cubase SX/SL 3 Power!* published by Course Technology (**www.courseptr.com**).

The project is set to loop the playback around the 2 bar MIDI part. Start the playback of the project to hear the a1 synth.

By default, the a1 will load with a bass synthesizer sound. We are going to change the patch to something that is more appropriate for the MIDI part in the project.

NOTE

Patch

A *patch* refers to the sound that the instrument is playing. The a1 (like most VST instruments) contains several preset patches that create a variety of sounds. You can use these presets or you can adjust the various controls of the a1 to create your own sound.

1. **Click** on the **Edit VST Instrument button**. The a1 will reappear on the screen.

> ## NOTE
>
> ### Grayed Out Option?
>
> Clicking on the Edit VST Instrument button will open the Edit window of the instrument connected to that MIDI track. If the track is not connected to a VST instrument, this option will be grayed out (unavailable).

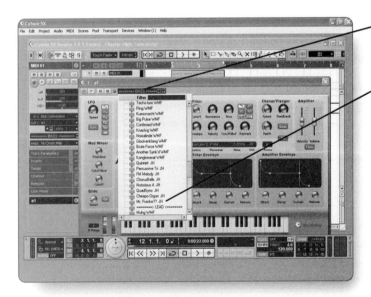

2. **Click** on the **Preset menu** from the a1 synth. The Preset drop-down menu will appear.

3. **Scroll** through the **list** of presets and **double-click** on the **Mr. Franke?? JH patch**. The a1 will now begin playing a synth line that will match the part being played in the project.

Freezing VST Instruments

Of course, this powerful technology comes with a price: VST instruments use the CPU to create their sounds, and in many cases a single instrument can place a heavy load on your computer. Imagine if you tried to work with several instruments at once; you could easily overload your machine. For this reason, Steinberg added the Freeze feature. This feature turns the MIDI track into a temporary audio track, since audio tracks consume far less CPU than VST instruments. Once you have a MIDI track edited and tweaked the way you like it, you can freeze it so that the instrument will release its CPU consumption. If after freezing an instrument you decide that you would like to go back and continue tweaking, you can unfreeze the instrument to continue editing.

Freezing the Instrument

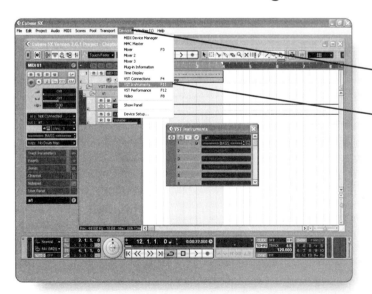

Let's begin by freezing the a1 VST instrument.

1. Click on the **Devices menu**. The Devices menu will appear.

2. Click on **VST instruments**. The VST Instruments rack window will appear.

TIP

VST Instrument Shortcut

Remember that you can open the VST Instrument rack window by pressing F11.

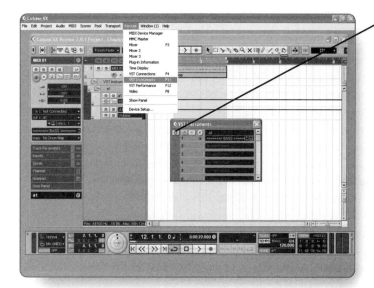

3. Click on the **Freeze button**. The Freeze Instrument Options dialog box will open.

TIP

Freeze

The Freeze feature will use the project's length to determine how much of the project to freeze (how long the temporary files will be). Before freezing an instrument, be sure to have the project length set to the correct length. If the project is too long, the freezing process will take longer.

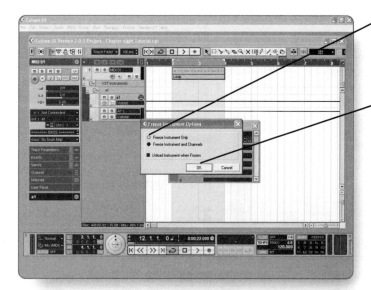

4. Click on the **circle** beside Freeze Instrument Only. You also have the option of freezing both the channel and the instrument.

5. Click on **OK**. The dialog box will close and the instrument will now be frozen.

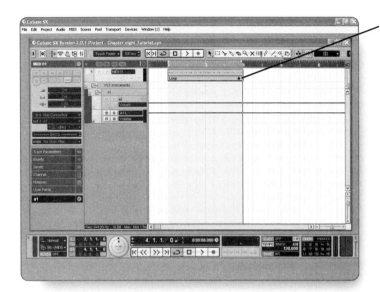

- Once the instrument is frozen, the MIDI track that was connected to it becomes locked. When locked, you cannot perform any edits to the MIDI track. If you want to apply further edits to the MIDI track, you will need to first unfreeze the instrument (see next section).

Unfreezing an Instrument

As mentioned, when an instrument is frozen, any MIDI tracks that are connected to it will be locked from any further editing. If you want to perform additional editing to the track, you will need to unfreeze the instrument first.

If the VST Instrument rack window is not on your screen, you will need to open it.

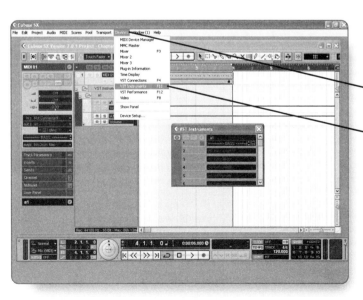

1. Click on the **Devices menu**. The Devices menu will appear.

2. Click on **VST Instruments**. The VST Instruments rack window will appear.

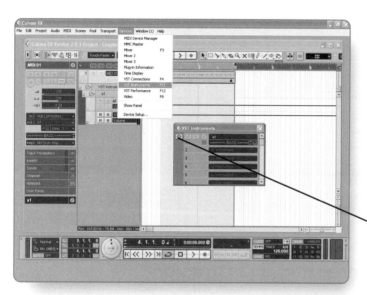

TIP

Toggling Windows

Some of the open windows might be covered by the project window. You can check which windows are open by clicking on the Windows menu. All open windows will appear at the bottom of the menu; simply click the one you want to view.

3. Click on the **Freeze button**. A dialog box will appear confirming that you want to unfreeze the instrument.

NOTE

Freeze Check

If you are not sure whether an instrument is frozen, use the Freeze button on the VST Instrument rack window as your indicator. If the button is orange, the track is currently frozen.

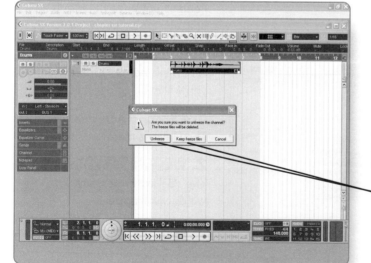

4. Click on **Unfreeze**. The Freeze function will become disabled and the track will become unlocked.

9

Getting to Know the Mixer

Did you know that Cubase can actually take the place of most hardware that can be found in a commercial recording studio? So far we have learned how to use SX like a tape machine to record both audio and MIDI performances. We also learned how to edit these performances, but this is not where the possibilities end. SX is also capable of mixing your song to perfection. Using the Mixer in SX, you can adjust the levels of each track to blend all the tracks together, as well as pan tracks left or right to create a stereo image.

In this chapter, you'll learn how to:

- Adjust channel volumes and panning
- Mute and solo channels
- Customize the Mixer with the different views

> **NOTE**
>
> **Tutorial**
>
> For the exercises in this chapter, you'll need to load the mixing tutorial project from www.courseptr.com/downloads. If you can't access the tutorial, then you will have to load your own recordings to mix.

Adjusting Channel Volumes and Panning

Perhaps the most common uses for the Mixer are to balance the volume of the tracks in your project and adjust the panning of a track to the left or right to create a stereo image. To demonstrate these functions, we'll perform a basic mix by adjusting the levels and panning of each track.

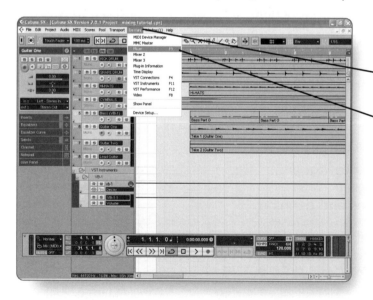

Start by opening the Mixer window.

1. **Click** on the **Devices menu**. The Devices menu will appear.

2. **Click** on **Mixer**. The Mixer will appear.

> **TIP**
>
> **Mixer Shortcut**
>
> You can also open the Mixer window by pressing F3.

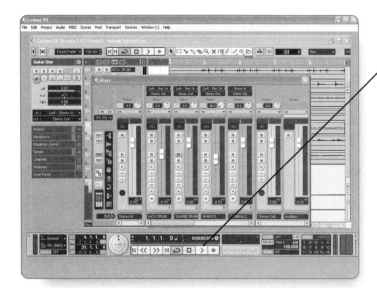

Next, let's adjust some of the tracks' volumes.

1. Click on the **Play button**. Playback will begin.

NOTE

Loop

This tutorial project is set to automatically loop; when the project reaches the end, it will loop back to the beginning and continue playing. There is no need to stop, rewind, and start the project again. This allows you to concentrate on working with the Mixer.

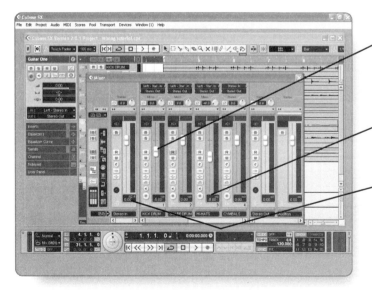

First, let's adjust the drum levels.

2. Click and drag the **kick drum channel's fader** down to around –5db. The level of the kick will decrease.

- The level of each fader is displayed just below the fader.

- This number indicates the peak level that the track has reached. This level will remain the same until a higher peak occurs. If you change the track's volume, this value will reset itself momentarily until it once again detects the highest peak of the track.

3. Shift + click and drag the **hi-hats fader** to about –8db. The level of the hi-hats will decrease.

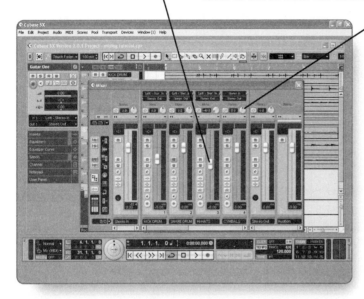

4. Shift + click and drag the **hi-hats channel's pan control** to the right until the pan value is about –40db. The hi-hats will now be mostly on the right side of the stereo field. Next let's create a stereo image with the guitars. You may have to expand the window or use the scroll buttons in the Mixer window to be able to view the guitars.

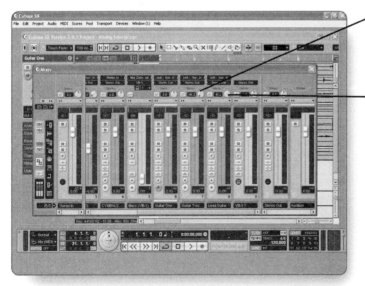

5. Shift + click and drag guitar one's pan control all the way to the left. Guitar one will now be on the left side.

6. Shift + click and drag guitar two's pan control all the way to the right. Guitar two will now be on the right side.

Now that you are comfortable adjusting levels and panning channels, try adjusting some of the other tracks' volumes and panning until you find all tracks are blending nicely.

Muting and Soloing Channels

In some situations, you might want to mute a channel so you can listen to the entire mix without it, or you may want to solo a channel so that you can focus on it.

Muting and Soloing Individual Channels

To demonstrate, we will mute then unmute the kick drum.

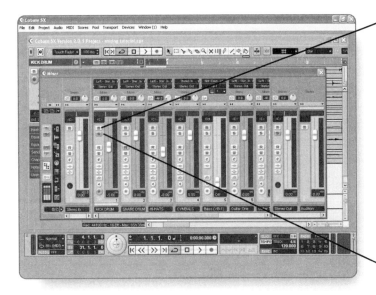

1. **Click** on the **M button** on the kick drum channel. The M button will become yellow and you will not be able to hear the kick drum in the mix.

2. **Click** on the **M button** again. The button will become inactive and you will once again hear the kick drum.

Next, let's solo the drum channel so that it is the only channel we hear.

3. **Click** on the **S button** on the kick drum channel. The button will turn red and all other channels will automatically become muted.

4. **Click** on the **S button** again. The solo will become deactivated.

NOTE

If you click on the Mute button of a channel that was muted when Solo was engaged, that channel will automatically become soloed as well.

Global Unmute and Unsolo

In some cases when mixing, you may have muted several tracks; in such a situation, going through every channel to unmute each one could be a tedious task. That's where the Global Unmute feature comes in. This unmutes all channels on which mute is active. There are actually two defeats—one for mute and one for solos.

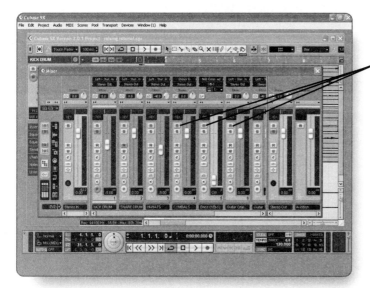

To begin, we'll need to mute several tracks.

1. **Click** on the **Mute button** for the guitar one, guitar two, and lead guitar channels. You will no longer be able to hear the guitars.

Now to unmute all the channels with one click, use the Defeat function.

2. **Click** on the **Mute Defeat button**. All the channels you muted will become unmuted.

NOTE

In this exercise, we used the Global Unmute feature to deactivate the mute on several channels; the same can be done with the Global Unsolo feature to deactivate all active solos.

Mixer Channel Views

In our mixing tutorial project, there are only a few tracks; this will make navigating the Mixer fairly easy. However, a situation may arise in which you are working with a large number of tracks, both MIDI and audio. In large mixes, moving around the Mixer can become confusing, since most of the channels look the same. This is where Mixer views come in. Mixer views allow you to customize which channels are displayed in the Mixer. Once you have set the Mixer's view the way you like it, you can save it as a Mixer view preset for quick recall at any time. This way you can create several presets to help your workflow—for example, one preset to view MIDI channels only and another to view audio channels.

NOTE

Track vs. Channels

When working in the Mixer window, an audio track is referred to as an audio channel (same for a MIDI track). The term "track" refers to a track in the project window that can have information (MIDI or audio) recorded or imported to it. However, a channel can be more than a track; it can also be an effect channel or group channel (more on effect channels and group channels in Chapter 10).

Hiding Channels

Let's begin customizing the Mixer by hiding some of the channels. In this project, there are three channel types: MIDI, audio, and the output of the VB-1 virtual instrument. We are going to create a Mixer view so that the Mixer will show only the audio channel types.

Let's begin by hiding the MIDI and VST instrument channels.

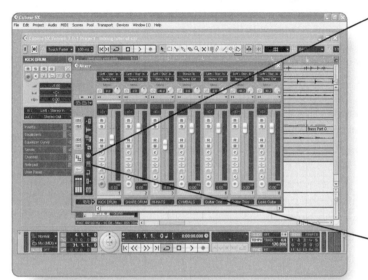

1. **Click** on the **Hide MIDI Channels button**. The MIDI channels will be removed from the Mixer.

> ### NOTE
> A channel that's hidden will be indicated by its Hide Channel button being illuminated in orange.

2. **Click** on **Hide VST Instruments**. The VB-1 instrument channel will be removed.

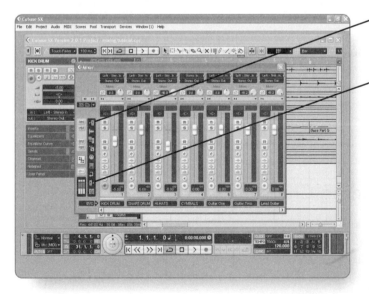

3. **Click** on **Hide Input Channels**. The input channels will be removed from the Mixer.

4. **Click** on **Hide Output Channels**. The output channels will be removed from the Mixer.

> ### NOTE
> To make a channel reappear in the Mixer, simply click on the Hide Channel button again.

Now the Mixer will show only the audio channels.

Saving and Recalling Mixer View Presets

Once you have the Mixer the way you like it, you can save the view as a preset so that it quickly can be recalled at anytime. This can be helpful if you want to quickly change the Mixer view to show only certain channel types, and it makes switching between the views a snap!

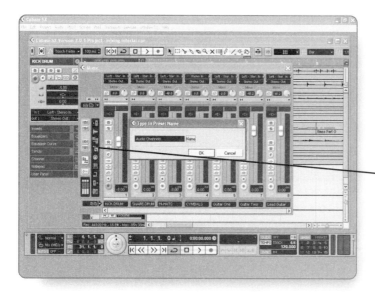

Saving a Preset

In the previous exercise, we hid the MIDI and VST instruments' channels, as well as the input and output channels. Next, we'll hide all remaining channels, except for the audio channels.

1. Click on all remaining **channel types**, except the audio channels, to hide them from the Mixer.

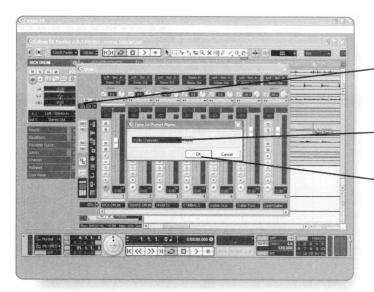

Next, let's save the view as a preset.

2. Click on the **Store View Set**. The Preset Name dialog window will appear.

3. Type Audio Channels in the Name field.

4. Click on **OK**. The view will be stored as a preset.

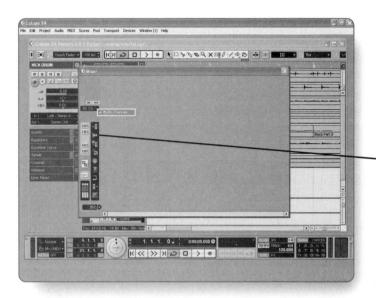

Recalling a Preset

Once you have your preset saved, you can quickly recall the Mixer view. To demonstrate recalling presets, we are going to begin by hiding all the channels.

1. **Click** on the **Hide Audio Channels button**. The audio channels will be removed from the Mixer.

NOTE

At this point, there should be no channels visible in the Mixer.

Now let's recall the audio channels preset.

2. **Click** on the **Select Channel View Set menu**. The drop-down menu of available presets will appear.

3. **Click** on **Audio Channels** from the list. The audio channels will appear in the Mixer.

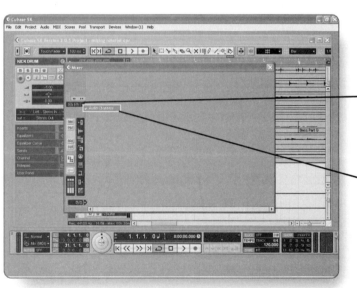

TIP

Using the previous exercise, you can easily create similar presets for each channel type; simply substitute the audio channel with a different channel type. Repeat the exercise until you have created a preset for each channel type.

10

Applying EQ and Effects

In the last chapter, we began to learn about mixing a project. You learned to balance the levels of each channel to create a nice blend between the tracks; you also learned to pan the channels to create a stereo image of the instruments. This is the basic starting point when mixing a project. In this chapter, we are going to take the next step in the mixing process, using EQs and applying effects. Equalizers (EQs) are used to boost or lower certain frequencies of an audio recording. This can be helpful to make one track stand out from the others. Effects can be used to enhance and add shine to your mixes by adding a special character to the tracks in the projects. For instance, when you're listening to a mix, you may think, "the guitars sound too close." You can add some distance to them by using a reverb. If the bass sounds too thin, trying adding some chorus.

In this chapter, you'll learn how to:

- Apply EQ to a channel
- Insert an effect to a channel
- Create and work with FX channels
- Apply offline effects

Applying EQ to a Channel

Almost everyone has used an equalizer at some point in his life. Have you ever seen a small radio with a "tone" control? Turning that knob to the left probably enhanced the lower tones, and turning it to the right most likely enhanced the higher tones. And that is essentially what an EQ does. With an EQ, you can increase or decrease frequencies of an audio recording or output of a VST instrument. Why might you want to do this? Sometimes two or more recordings may have a similar frequency response. For example, when a bass guitar and a kick drum are mixed together, it can sometimes be hard for the ear to separate the two. By using an EQ, you can adjust the frequencies in order to help separate the two instruments.

As with most operations in SX, there are several ways to apply EQ. For the purpose of this book, we'll be using the Audio Channels Settings window to apply EQ to the kick drum.

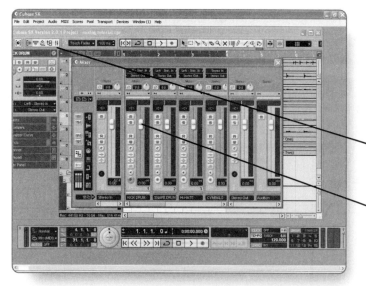

> **NOTE**
>
> **Tutorial**
>
> For this chapter, we'll be continuing to work with the mixing tutorial project. If you don't have access to the tutorial you can use your own recordings.

To open the Channel Settings window:

1. **Click** on the **Mixer button** in the task bar. The Mixer will appear.

2. **Click** on the **e button** on the kick drum channel. The Channel Settings window will appear.

NOTE

Mixer Button Missing?

If you do not see the Mixer button in the task bar, you can open it by right-clicking on the task bar and then selecting View Switches.

Next we are going to apply EQ. For this exercise we will EQ the kick drum in order to separate it from the bass guitar, sonically.

Let's start by EQing the frequencies around 500Hz.

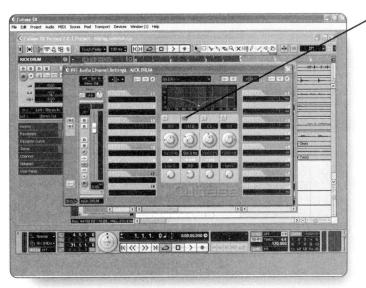

1. **Click** on band two's **Lo-Mid Enable button**. The button will become green to indicate that band two is enabled.

NOTE

Bands

SX's EQ consists of four bands; one band will allow you to control one frequency. This means you can boost or cut up to four different frequencies with a single EQ. For this example, we are going to be using just two of the four bands. There are no hard and fast rules when using an EQ; this example is to demonstrate how to use SX's built-in EQ. Feel free to experiment further.

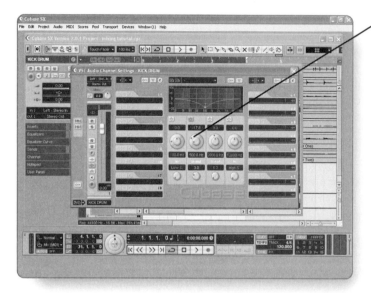

2. **Turn** the **Lo-Mid Frequency knob** to a setting of around 500Hz.

TIP

Manually Entering Settings

You can also double-click on the Values field of the EQ to enter the setting manually.

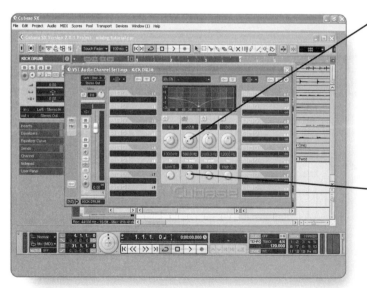

3. **Turn** the **Lo-Mid Gain knob** to the right. The level of the frequency around 500Hz will begin to increase. **Set** the **gain level** to around 8db. Looking at the EQ's display, you will notice what appears to be a small hill with a 2 on the very top of the hill.

4. **Turn** the **Lo-Mid Q knob** to the right to a value of about 3db. The width of the hill will decrease. The width of the EQ controls the amount for frequencies around 500Hz that will be affected by the boost or cut in level.

Now the kick drum will have a slightly higher tone to it, which will help separate it from the bass guitar.

Next we'll reduce some of the high frequencies. While this may not help separate the kick drum from the bass guitar, it will help separate the kick from some of the tracks with higher frequencies, such as the hi-hats and cymbals.

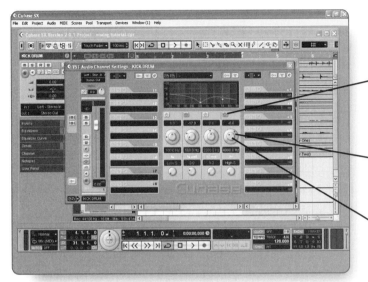

1. **Click** on the **Hi Band Enable button**. The button will turn green indicating that the band is enabled.

2. **Turn** the **Hi Band's frequency knob** to the right and set it to about 5000Hz.

3. **Turn** the **Gain knob** to the left to about –8db. The EQ display will now show a small downward slope starting around 1000Hz.

Now the higher frequencies are being gradually reduced; this will allow the tracks with a large number of high frequencies to shine through a little more.

Inserting an Effect on a Channel

Next, we'll look at using effects to add a touch of color to our project. Cubase SX comes loaded with several different effects that will allow you to create professional-sounding mixes; however, for the purposes of this book, we are not going to cover the details of each effect. We'll be looking at the various methods of adding the effects to your projects and how to mix with them.

We'll begin with Insert effects. An Insert effect is placed at the top of a channel where the audio will pass through and continue to the rest of channel EQ and channel volume control. What comes out of the inserted effect will of course not be the same as what goes in.

Each channel in the Mixer has eight insert slots, so in theory, you can have your audio track or VST instrument pass through eight effects before it reaches the channel's EQ and volume control. There are a few different ways you can insert an effect. We are going to look at two.

To demonstrate, we are going to insert a Reverb effect on the snare drum.

> ## NOTE
>
> ### Reverb Definition
>
> Reverb is a type of effect that is used to re-create different listening environments by emulating the sonic characteristics of a particular room or space.

1. Click on the **Mixer button** from the task bar. The Mixer will appear.

2. Click on the **e button** on the snare drum channel. The Channel Settings window will appear.

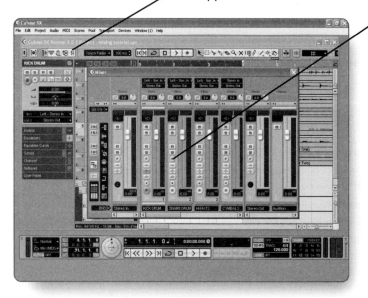

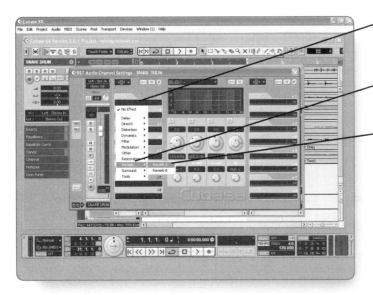

3. Click on **insert slot one**. A drop-down menu with available effects will appear.

4. Click on **Reverb**. The Reverb submenu will appear.

5. Click on **Reverb A**. The effect's window will appear.

Now we are going to choose a preset that will go nicely with the snare drum.

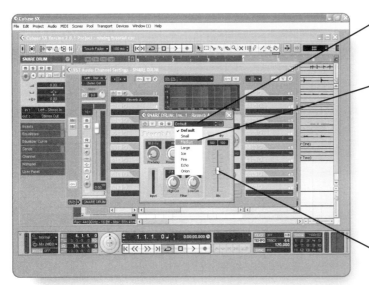

1. Click on the **Preset field**. A drop-down menu of available presets will appear.

2. Click on **Medium**. The snare drum will now have a mild amount of reverb to it.

Next let's adjust the reverb level. Since the snare is passing through the effect, we must adjust the level in the effect itself.

3. Drag the **Mix fader** up and the level of reverb will decrease; drag the fader down and the reverb's level will increase.

NOTE

Adjusting Reverb Mix

When adjusting the mix in the Reverb interface, you are not actually changing the level of the audio on that channel. You are adjusting the balance between the unaffected and affected audio.

Next we'll take a look at how to remove an inserted effect.

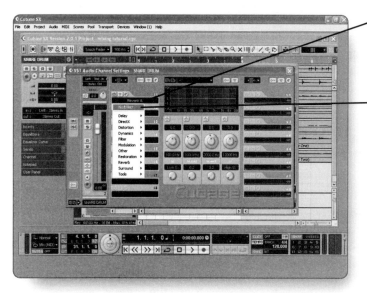

1. Click on **insert slot one** from the Channel Settings window. The Insert pop-up menu will appear.

2. Click on **No Effect**. The effect will be removed from the channel.

NOTE

Discarding Changes

Because we made some changes to the Reverb effect's settings, when you remove the effect, a pop-up dialog window will appear asking you to confirm your decision to discard the effect's changes. Click Discard to continue.

Working with FX Channels

Inserting effects is only one method of applying effects to your audio or VST instrument channels. One limitation of inserting effects is that, used in that way, they can be applied to only one channel at a time. There may be a situation in which you want to add the same effect to multiple channels; for example, applying the same Reverb effect to each channel that makes up the drum kit. In such a situation, you will be using the FX channels. When using FX channels, you will send a portion of an audio or a VST instrument channel to an effect. Using FX channels, it is possible to apply the effect to several channels at the same time.

To demonstrate, we'll be creating an FX channel in our tutorial project and sending a portion of each of the drum channels to the effect.

Begin by adding an FX channel:

1. **Click** on the **Project menu**. The Project menu will appear.

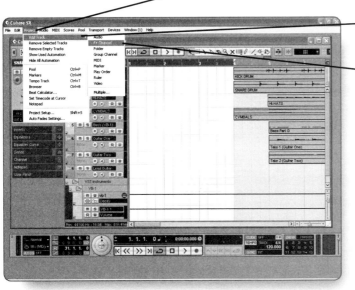

2. **Click** on **Add Track**. The Add Track submenu will appear.

3. **Click** on **FX Channel**. The Add FX Channel dialog window will appear.

● **Configuration**. This menu will allow you to choose the output type of the FX channel. There are several configurations available, such as stereo and mono; in addition, there are several modes for surround sound mixing. For our exercise, we'll use the stereo setting.

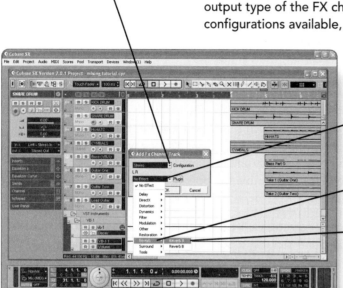

4. **Click** on the **Plug-in menu**. The drop-down menu of available effects will appear.

5. **Click** on **Reverb**. The Reverb submenu will appear.

6. **Click** on **Reverb A**. The Reverb effect will be added to the Plug-in menu.

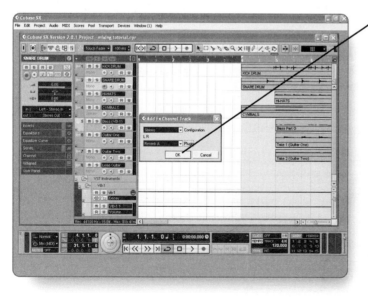

7. **Click** on **OK**. The FX channel will appear in the project window (and the Mixer window). And the effect Reverb A will appear on the screen.

Next let's rename the FX channel to something that will make it easier for us to recognize. Because we are going to send all the drum tracks to this FX channel, we'll use Drum FXs as the channel name.

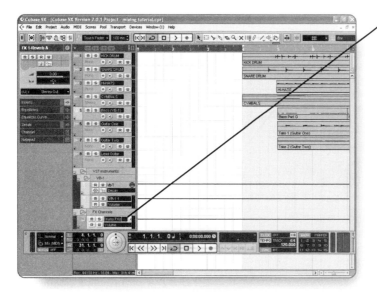

1. Double-click on the **FX channel's name**. The name will become highlighted.

2. Type Drums FXs and **press Enter**. The FX will now be renamed.

Extending the Mixer

Next we have to send our drum channels to the effect. To do this, we need to extend the Mixer. When the Mixer is extended, we can access other settings of the Mixer channels without having to open the Channels Settings window.

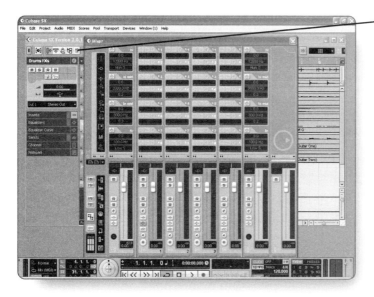

1. Click on the **Mixer button** from the task bar. The Mixer will appear.

TIP

Mixer Shortcut

Remember you can also open the Mixer by pressing F3.

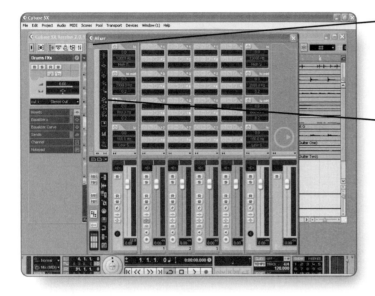

2. Click on the **Show Extend Mixer button**. The Mixer will extend its height to reveal additional settings for each channel.

3. Click on the **Show All Sends button**. The send settings for each channel will appear.

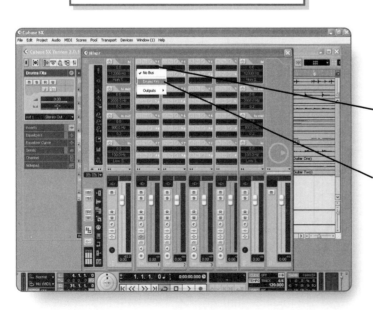

Next we are going to send one of each drum track to the Reverb B that we just added to the FX channel.

4. Click on **send one** on the kick drum channel. A pop-up menu will appear.

5. Click on **Drums FXs**. The send will now be set to route to the FX channel.

CAUTION

Renaming the Channel

If you did not rename the FX channel as described previously, the FX channel will not be displayed as "Drums FXs."

Next we need to enable the sends and increase the send level.

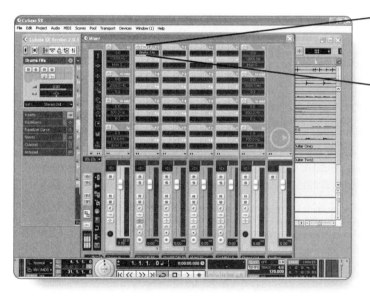

6. **Click** on the **Send Enable button** on the kick drum channel. The send will become active.

7. **Click and drag** the **send level** to about 50%. You will now hear the reverb being applied to the kick drum.

NOTE

Adjusting Send Level

Adjusting the level of the send will control how much of the drum channel is sent to the FX channel; increasing the level will increase the amount of effect that is applied.

TIP

Setting Amounts for Different Channels

When sending the drum tracks to the FX channel, each send does not have to be set to the same amount. Experiment with the send levels on each drum track until you find a balance you like.

8. **Repeat steps 4-7** for all the remaining drum tracks (snare drum, hi-hats, and cymbals) to send these tracks to the FX channel.

Offline Audio Processing

When using effects, either as inserts or in an FX channel, the effects are being applied to the audio tracks or VST instruments in real time; this means that the recordings are not being permanently altered, which allows you to freely apply effects as well as experiment with different effects without having to commit to any changes. But real-time effects are being processed by your computer's CPU during playback, and for every effect you use, the harder your computer has to work. For this reason SX has an Offline Processing feature. Offline processing allows you to permanently apply an effect to an audio recording. This might be helpful if you are working on a project in which your computer's resources are running low.

Applying Standard Audio Processing

Offline processing has two sections: One is used for applying basic functions, such as volume changes, fade ins, and fade outs, and the other is for processing effect plug-ins, such as reverbs and delays. We'll start our look at offline processing with the basic functions.

To demonstrate, we are going to change the volume of the hi-hats.

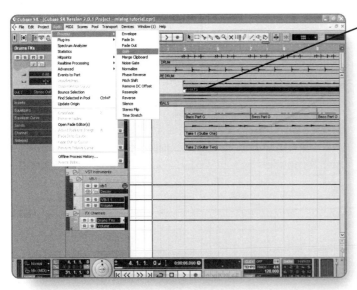

1. Click on the **hi-hats audio event** in the project window. The event will become highlighted.

> **TIP**
>
> **Organizing Windows**
> If you have several windows open, remember you can use the Window menu to quickly bring the project window to the front.

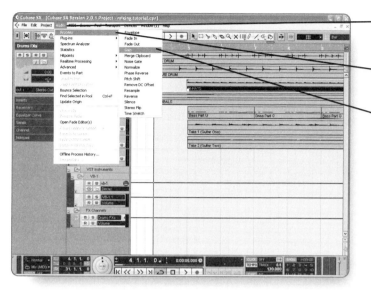

2. Click on the **Audio menu**. The Audio menu will appear.

3. Click on **Process**. The Process submenu will appear.

4. Click on **Gain**. The Gain dialog window will appear.

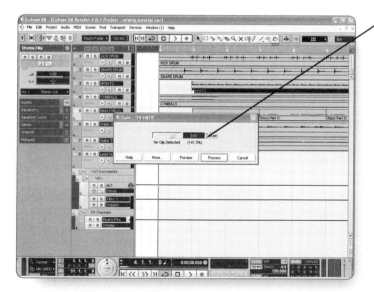

5. Click on the **Gain up arrow** three times. The Gain field will display 3.00; this shows that we'll be increasing the volume by 3db.

TIP

Previewing Results

Offline processing allows you to preview the results before you commit to the changes. To do so, simply click on the Preview button.

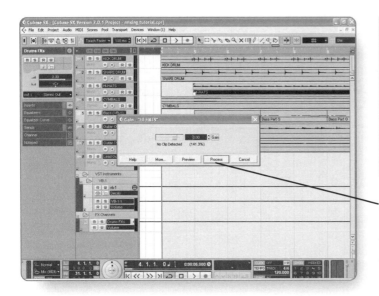

NOTE

Processing Functions

SX comes with several processing functions. For more information on each function, consult SX's documentation.

6. Click on **Process**. The Progress window will appear. When the process is complete, the hi-hats will now be 3db louder.

Applying Offline Audio Plug-ins

Next we are going to look at using offline processing to permanently apply effects to your audio recordings.

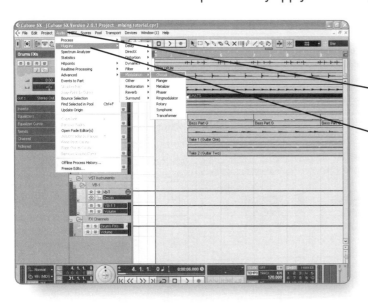

In the next exercise we'll be applying a chorus effect to the hi-hats.

1. Click on the **Audio**. The Audio menu will appear.

2. Click on **Plug-ins**. The Plug-in submenu will appear.

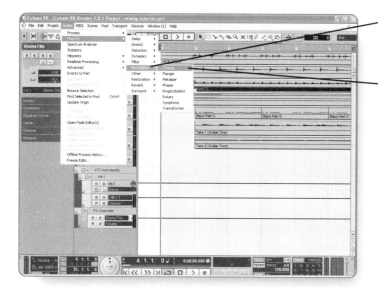

3. Click on **Modulation**. The Modulation group menu will appear.

4. Click on **Chorus**. The Chorus effect window will appear.

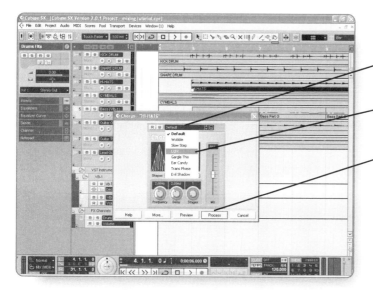

We are going to apply one of the chorus's presets.

5. Click on the **preset list**. The Preset menu will appear.

6. Click on **Light**. The preset will be loaded.

7. Click on **Process**. The progress window will appear; when it's complete the effect will be applied to the hi-hats.

TIP

Previewing Results

Remember you can preview the results prior to processing the effect.

NOTE

Undo Shortcut

If you have processed an audio track with an effect, and decided that you do not like the results, you can easily undo the processing by using "Undo" in the Edit menu, or by pressing Ctrl + Z (Command + Z for Macintosh users).

11

Automation and Mixing Tips

In this chapter you will learn to automate the movement of Mixer controls. Automation allows you to record any movements and adjustments made to most of the controls on the Mixer. This allows you to build a more dynamic mix. Do you have a guitar track that you want to be quiet in some parts of the project and louder in others? Use automation to record changes to the channel's volume control. Perhaps you want to automatically pan a track from left to right? Once again, automation will make this possible. We will also consider some of the other features in SX that will allow you to take further control of your mix.

In this chapter, you'll learn how to:

- Record Mixer automation
- Record EQ automation
- Use group channels and link Mixer channels together

Recording Mixer Movements

Let's begin our look at automation by recording some volume changes to our mixing tutorial. At bar 18, beat 1, the lead guitar plays a chord that is a tad too loud compared to the rest of the track. We are going to automate the volume on the guitar's channel so that it decreases while the chord is played, and then returns to its previous level when the chord is finished.

1. **Click** on the **W (Write) button** on the lead guitar channel. Automation write will be enabled on that channel.

2. **Click** on the **Play button**. Playback will begin.

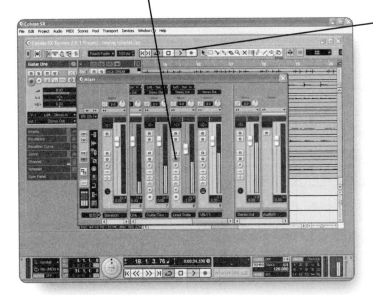

> ## NOTE
>
> ### Automation Location
>
> Be sure to start the project from any point before bar 18, since it is around this location that you'll be writing automation.

3. When the project cursor reaches just before the chord on bar 18, **click and drag** the **fader** down 3db. The volume of the lead guitar will decrease.

● The Mixer's level indicators will let you know how much you are decreasing the fader. For this exercise, we are reducing the guitar about 3db during the loud chord. This is not a hard and fast rule; feel free to experiment.

4. After the project cursor passes the chord, **click and drag** the **fader** back to its original level.

5. **Click** on the **Stop button**. The project will stop.

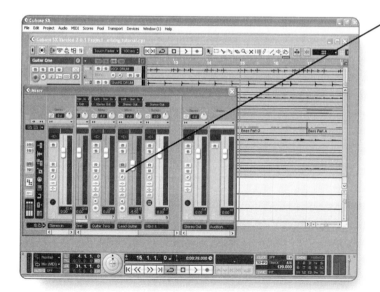

6. **Click** on the **Write button** on the lead guitar channel to disable automation writing. This is for safety, so that you don't accidentally record any unwanted changes.

CAUTION

Write Enabling Warning

When a channel has automation write enabled, any changes made to the channel during playback will be recorded. Unless you are planning to record changes to the channel, it's a good idea to keep Write mode disabled.

7. **Click** on the **R button**. Now the Mixer will follow the changes you recorded when the project is played.

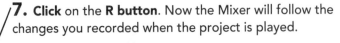

8. **Bring** the **project cursor** back to bar 15.

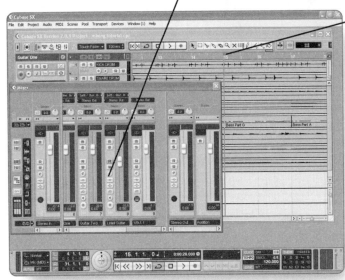

TIP

Playback Position Shortcut

Remember, you can move the cursor quickly to any location by clicking on the ruler above the project window. In addition, double-clicking on the ruler will begin playback from the point you clicked on the ruler.

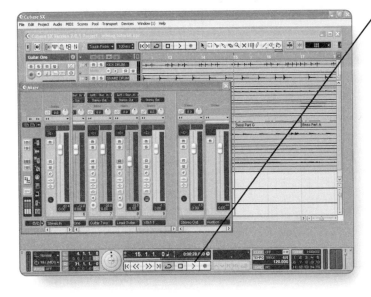

9. **Click** on the **Play button**. The project will begin its playback; when it reaches bar 18, the fader on the lead guitar channel will automatically decrease to –3db, and then when the loud chord passes, it will return to its original position.

Next let's record some changes to the panning of a channel. For this exercise we are going to pan the lead guitar so that parts of it are on the left side, while other parts will be on the right.

We'll begin by re-enabling the write automation on the lead guitar track.

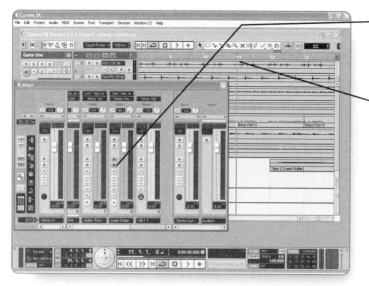

1. Click on the **Write automation button** on the lead guitar channel. Automation write will be enabled.

2. Click on the **ruler** at bar 11. The cursor will relocate to bar 11.

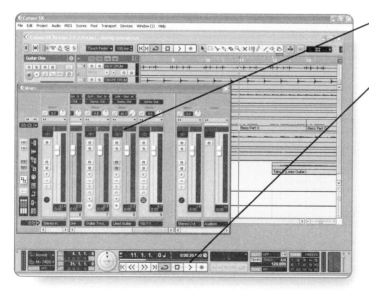

3. Click and drag the **pan** of the lead guitar channel to the full left position.

4. Click on the **Play button**. The project will begin to playback.

TIP

Mixer Window

If you have several windows open when recording automation, it is helpful to have the Mixer window in front prior to playing the project so you will be prepared to make the changes.

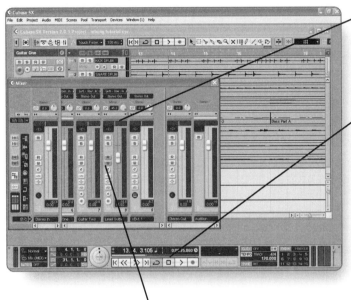

5. When the project cursor reaches bar 14, gradually **click and drag** the **pan** toward the right until you have reached the full right position.

6. Click on the **Stop button**. The project's playback will stop.

7. Click on the channel's **Write button**. Automation writing will be disabled.

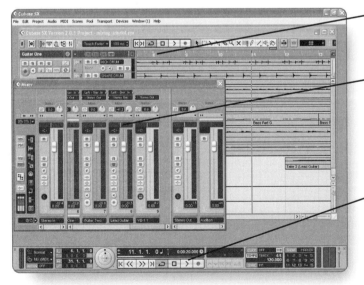

8. Click on the **ruler** at bar 11. The project cursor will relocate to bar 11.

● When the cursor relocates, you'll notice that the pan control has moved back to the left side, since this was its original location before the changes were recorded.

9. Click on the **Play button**. The project will play back. When the cursor reaches bar 14, the pan control will begin to move to the right just as you recorded it.

Automating the EQ

Just as we recorded changes to a channel's volume and pan, we can also record changes to the EQs. To demonstrate, we are going to use one band of the EQ to create an automated sweeping effect on the lead guitar.

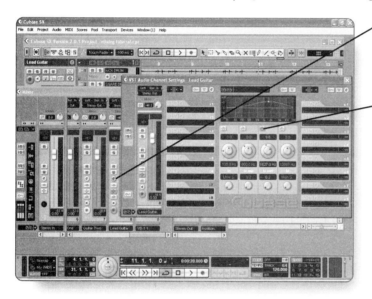

1. **Click** on the **Channel Settings button** for the lead guitar. The channel setting will appear.

2. **Click** on the **Hi-Mid button**. The hi-mid band will become enabled.

For the EQ to have an effect on the guitar you will need to increase or decrease the hi-mid band. For this exercise we'll be increasing the band.

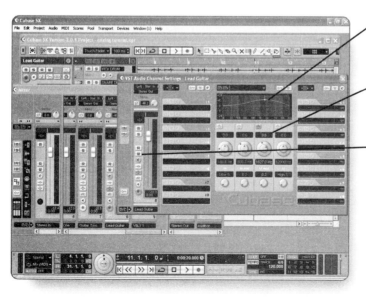

3. **Click** on the band's **frequency point** on the EQ graph and **drag** it **up** about 10db.

● Use the hi-mid band's gain display to guide you to a setting of 10db.

4. **Click** on the channel's **Automation Write button**. Automation write will become enabled.

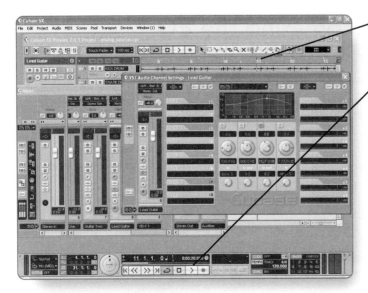

5. Click on **bar 11** on the ruler. The project cursor will relocate to bar 11.

6. Click on the **Play button**. The project will begin playback.

TIP

Playback Shortcut

When you are preparing to record automation, it is a good idea to use the spacebar key command to start playback. This way you do not need to move the mouse to the transport panel and back to the Mixer to make the changes.

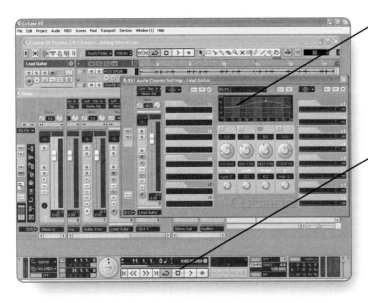

7. When you hear the lead guitar begin to play, **click and gradually drag** the band's **frequency setting** to the left. When you reach the end of the frequency range, **drag** it back to the **right**.

8. Click on the **Stop button** when you get back to the original position. The playback will stop.

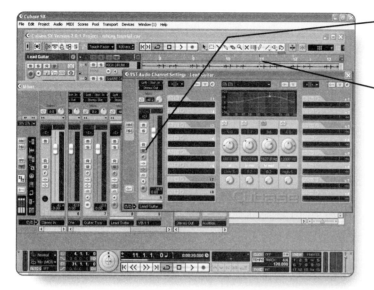

9. **Click** on the **Write Automation button**. Write automation will be disabled.

10. **Bring** the **project cursor** back to bar 11 and **click** on the **Play button**. The EQ will play back the changes you recorded.

Mixer Tips—Group Channels and Linking Channels

Two features that will help your workflow and creativity are group channels and channel linking. Both can be useful in many ways, such as applying the same effect to several channels or controlling the volume of several channels by adjusting one control.

Group Channels

Let's imagine a situation in which you are working on a mix of a drum kit. You have spent hours tweaking each piece of the kit, applying EQ, effects, and adjusting the levels. If, on listening, you feel that the drums are too loud, you could go back and adjust each piece of the kit again to bring down the volume, but then you would most likely have to tweak the mix again. A better idea would be to assign each drum channel to a group channel, and then you could just adjust the level of the group to set the overall level of the kit.

Let's demonstrate this by creating a group channel and grouping all the drum tracks to it.

First we need to create the group channel.

1. Click on the **Project menu**. The Project menu will appear.

2. Click on **Add Track**. The Add Track submenu will appear.

3. Click on **Group Channel**. The Add Group Channel Track window will appear.

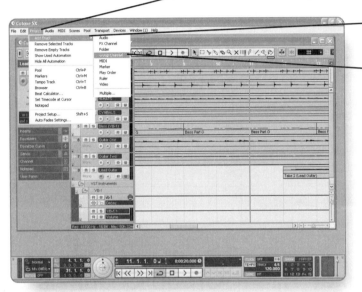

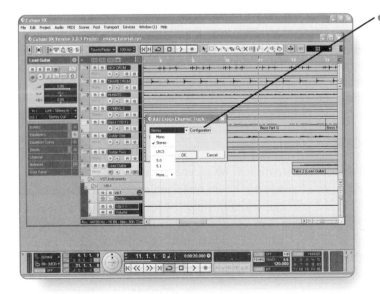

- **Configuration menu**. This menu allows you to select the type of group channel you want to add. For most cases in music production, you will be using a stereo or mono group channel. If you are going to be grouping channels that are panned both left and right, then you will need to use a stereo group. If you plan to group channels that are all panned either left or right, or even straight up in the center, you will need to use a mono group channel. For our example, we are going to use a stereo group channel, which is the default selection.

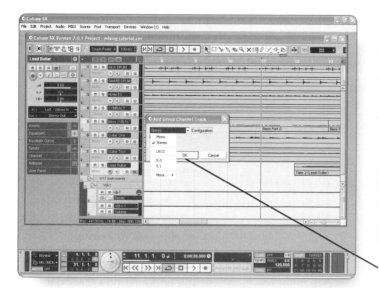

4. **Click** on **OK**. The group channel will be added to the project.

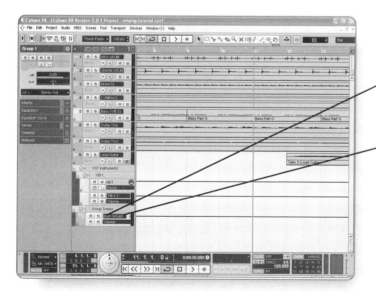

Next let's rename the group channel to something that will be easier to recognize.

5. **Double-click** on the group channel's **Name field**. The name will become highlighted.

6. **Type** in the name **Drum Group** and then **press Return**. The channel will change to the new name.

Next, from the Mixer, assign the output of the drum tracks to the group channel.

7. **Click once** to select the **kick drum**. It will be highlighted.

8. Click on the **kick drum's output**. The Output menu will appear.

9. **Click** on **Drum Group**. The kick drum's output will now be routed to the group channel.

10. **Repeat steps 7 and 8** for the remaining drum tracks (snare drum, hi-hats, and cymbals).

Now we can control the volume of the entire drum kit with one fader.

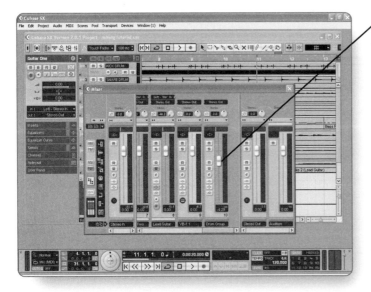

11. **Click and drag** the **Drum Group fader** up and down. You will notice how it affects the volume of all drum tracks.

NOTE

Grouping Benefit

Group channels also have effect inserts and sends just like the audio and VST instrument channels do; this makes it possible to apply an effect to the group (refer to Chapter 10 for working with effects).

Linking Channels

When channels are linked together, any changes made to a channel's fader will affect all the linked channel's faders. This can also be helpful when you want to quickly control the volume of several channels without having to use a group channel.

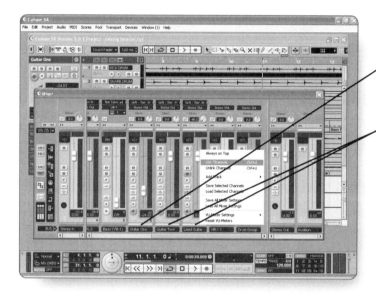

To begin, we need to select the channels that we want to link.

1. **Click** on the **channel selector** for the guitar one channel. The channel will become highlighted.

2. **Ctrl + click** (**Command + click** for Macintosh users) on the **channel selectors** for the guitar two and lead guitar channels. Now all three guitar channels will be selected.

TIP

Selecting Multiple Channels

Use Shift + cursor keys (left and right) to select multiple channels in the Mixer.

---

3. **Right-click** (**Control + click** for Macintosh users) on the **Mixer**. The Mixer's pop-up menu will appear.

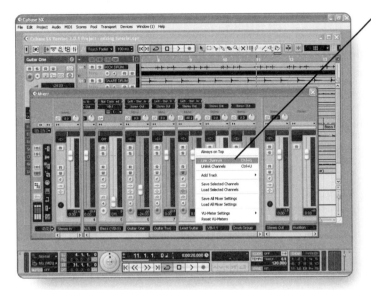

4. Click on **Link Channels**. The channels will now be linked.

> ### TIP
>
> #### Linking Channels Shortcut
>
> You can skip steps 3 and 4 by pressing Ctrl + G (Command + G for Macintosh users) to link channels together.

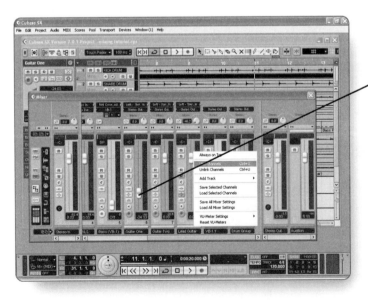

Now let's see how changes made to one fader will affect the others that are linked to it.

5. Click and drag the **fader** of guitar one. As you move the fader, the faders of the other guitar tracks will also move.

12

Finalizing Your Mix

After spending hours tweaking your mix to perfection, you will need to perform a mixdown. Performing a mixdown means going through the project and creating a single stereo file that includes all the audio tracks, VST instruments, level changes, automation, EQ, and effects. This final file can be burned to CD and replicated. You can even create an MP3 so you can share your song via the Internet.

In this chapter, you'll learn how to:

- Perform a mixdown to a stereo file
- Create an MP3 file of your project

Performing a Mixdown

Your mixdown file will include all the effects, automation, and other changes you made to your project while mixing. In this chapter, we will be mixing down the tutorial project we have been working with. Again, it's not necessary to use this file; you can use any of your own recordings.

We will begin by setting the left and right locators. Anything between these locators will be included in the mixdown file; therefore, be sure to set them around everything that you want to hear in the final stereo file.

1. Press **Shift + F** to zoom out full over the project.

2. Place the **pointer** on top of the project ruler at bar 4. The point will become a pencil.

3. Click and drag on the **ruler** from bar 4 to bar 31. The locators will be set so that the entire project is within the blue locator's range.

With the locators set, we can now create the mixdown.

TIP

Placing Locators

By selecting the kick drum event and using the P key command, the left and right locators automatically will be placed around the kick drum event. This can be helpful when setting the locators for a mixdown; however, when using this command be sure to select an event or audio part that is long enough so that the entire project will be included in the mixdown. You can press Ctrl + A to select all the parts and events on the project prior to using the P command to set the locators. This will ensure that the locators will include all parts.

---

4. Click on the **File menu**. The File menu will appear.

5. Place your **mouse** on Export. The Export submenu will appear.

6. Click on **Audio Mixdown**. The Export Audio Mixdown window will appear.

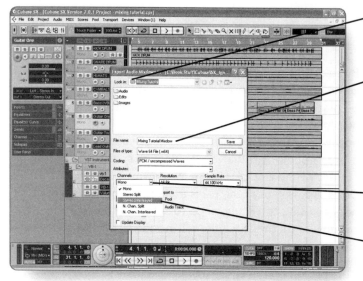

7. **Navigate** to the **folder** on your hard disk in which you want to save the mixdown file.

8. **Type** in **Mixing Tutorial Mixdown** (this will be the name of the mixdown file).

Next we need to adjust some of the settings.

9. **Click** on the **Channels menu**. The Channels menu will appear.

10. **Click** on **Stereo Inter-leaved**. A stereo interleaved file is one file containing both left and right channels.

NOTE

Stereo or Mono

The channel setting allows you to choose whether you want the mixdown to be in stereo or mono. When creating a stereo mix, you have two options: The first option—Stereo Split—creates two separate mono files, one file for the left channel and one for the right. The second—Stereo Interleaved—creates a single file with both left and right channels combined into a single file. For most situations, you will want to mixdown to a Stereo Interleaved file.

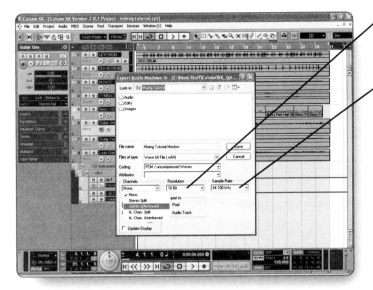

11. Click on the **Resolution menu** and **select 16 Bit** from the drop-down menu.

12. Click on the **Sample Rate menu** and **select 44.100 kHz** from the drop-down menu.

> **NOTE**
>
> **CD Resolution**
>
> If this mix will end up on CD, the resolution and sample rate need to be 16-bit and 44.1kHz, respectively.

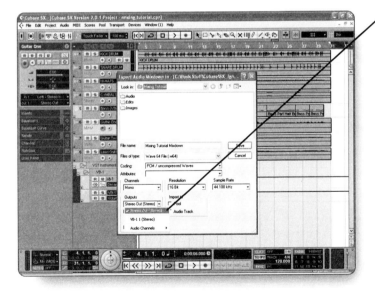

13. Click on the **Outputs menu** and **select Stereo Out**.

> **NOTE**
>
> **Multiple Busses**
>
> If you are working with more than one bus in the Cubase Mixer, or working with custom busses, please consult your SX documentation or *Cubase SX/SL 3 Power!* by Robert Guerin.

NOTE

Select Output

SX will use the audio that is routed to one of its outputs to create the file. In most cases, you will have just one output enabled (Stereo Out); for this reason, you should select this output when performing a mixdown. Consult SX's documentation if you are going to be working with more than one stereo output.

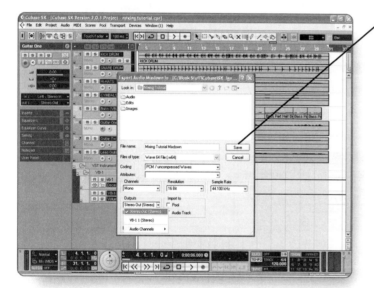

14. Click on **Save**. SX will begin mixing down the project.

CAUTION

Outboard Devices

If you are using any outboard MIDI devices, such as synthesizers or drum machines, these devices will not be included with the mixdown. The mixdown process will only include outputs of audio tracks, effect return tracks, and MIDI tracks that drive internal VST instruments. If you want to include outboard MIDI devices in your mixdown, they must first be converted to audio.

Creating an MP3 File

With the boom in popularity of the MP3 format, musicians are now able to share their finished mixes through the Internet. Not only does the MP3 format make the mixdown file small enough to send via the Net, you can also add ID3 tags to the file. Tags allow you to include additional information such as artist name, song name, album, and genre. Most players will display this information while playing the song.

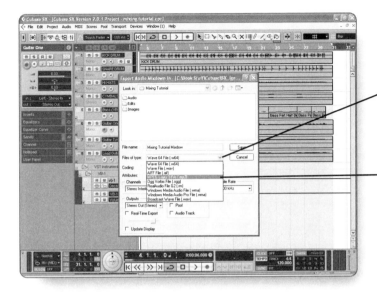

Let's create an MP3 mixdown file.

1. Follow steps 1-13 of the preceding mixdown exercise.

2. Click on the **Files of Type menu** (**Format menu** for Macintosh users). A drop-down menu will appear.

3. Click on **MPEG Layer 3 File (.mp3)**. It will be selected.

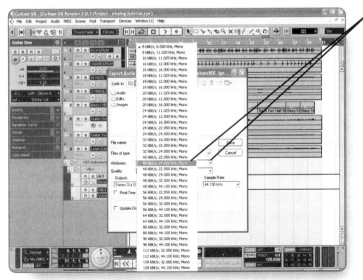

4. Click on the **Attributes drop-down menu** and **select** the desired **MP3 bit rate**.

NOTE

Using a larger bit rate will give you a better-sounding MP3; however, the MP3 file will be larger. Experiment with the different bit rates until you find a good balance between size and quality. Typically a setting of 160 kBits/sec; 44.100kHz; Stereo should be adequate.

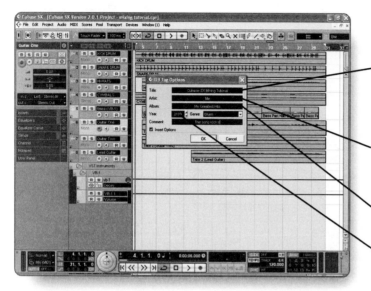

5. Click on **Save**. The MP3 ID3 Tags window will appear.

- **Title**. Enter the name of your song; for this exercise, let's call it Cubase SX Mixing Tutorial.

- **Artist**. Here you would enter your name, unless of course it is somebody else's song.

- **Album**. Enter the name of the album.

- **Year**. Set the year the song was made.

- **Genre**. Use the Genre drop-down menu to select the genre that the song matches.

- **Comment**. Insert any comments that you want to add to the song's tags.

- **Insert Options**. If this check box is ticked, the tags will be written with the MP3 file; if it is unchecked, then no tags will be written.

6. Click on **OK**. The mixdown to MP3 will begin.

13

Customizing Cubase

SX has a well-designed user interface that is intuitive and makes working in the program a breeze, but it does not stop there. SX allows you to customize the program to make it look and feel the way you want it. You can apply changes to the user interface as well as to parts of your project.

In this chapter, you'll learn how to:

- Customize the transport panel
- Colorize parts and events
- Customize the toolbar
- Customize SX's startup

Customizing the Transport Panel

Let's begin customizing SX by adding and removing components from the transport panel. One of the neat things about customizing the transport panel is that a few presets have been included, allowing you to quickly alter the look of the transport. In addition, you can pick and choose which components are visible.

Using Transport Preset Views

The good folks at Steinberg have added some preset views to the transport panel; these presets will allow you to quickly change the look of the transport panel by simply clicking on the preset name.

To change presets:

1. **Right-click** (**Control + click** for Macintosh users) on the **transport panel**. The Transport Components pop-up menu will appear.

2. **Select Transport Buttons** from the pop-up menu. The transport panel will change so that it displays only the transport buttons.

To restore the transport panel to its default settings, follow these steps.

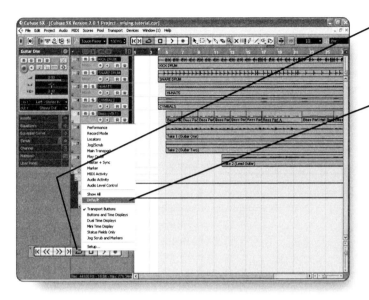

3. Right-click (**Control + click** for Macintosh users) on the **transport**. The Transport Components menu will appear.

4. Click on **Default**. The transport will restore itself to the default setting.

Repeat this exercise a few times, choosing a different preset each time so you will become familiar with the available presets.

Customizing the Components

In addition to the presets, you can also pick and choose which of the components are visible on the transport bar.

To demonstrate, let's remove some of the components.

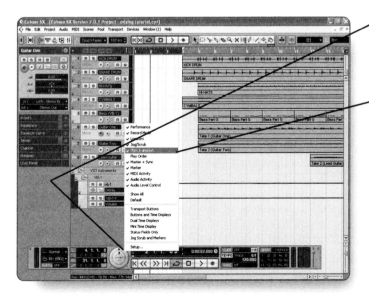

1. Right-click (**Control + click** for Macintosh users) on the **transport**. The Transport Components menu will appear.

2. Click on **Main Transport**. The transport buttons will be removed.

Next we'll restore the transport buttons.

3. Right-click (**Control + click** for Macintosh users) on the **transport**. The Transport Components menu will appear.

4. Click on **Main Transport**. The transport buttons will return to the transport panel.

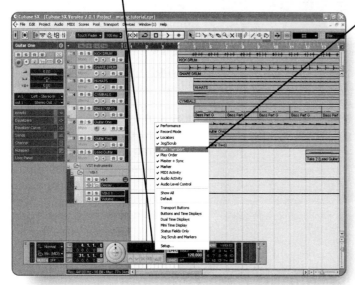

> ## NOTE
> ### Checkmark
> A checkmark next to a component in the menu indicates that the component is visible.

Again, it is a good idea to repeat this exercise and choose a different component each time to become familiar with all of the components.

Colorizing Parts or Events

If you're working with a project that has many tracks, it can be difficult to keep the tracks organized. Cubase helps by allowing you to assign a different color to each event or part on each track. For example, you can color guitars orange, vocals green, and so on. Or, you can color various sections of the song a particular color.

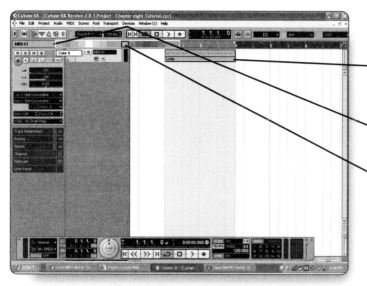

Using our tutorial project, let's color the drum event blue.

1. **Click** on any **event** to select it. The drum event will become highlighted.

2. **Click** on the **Color Selector menu**. The menu will appear.

3. **Click** on **Color 9** (light blue). The event will become blue.

TIP

Coloring Multiple Parts

You can also select multiple parts or events in the project window to apply the same color to each part or event.

NOTE

Creating Colors

At the bottom of the Color Selector menu, you will find the Select Colors option; use this to edit the available colors or to create your own color.

Customizing the Task Bar

The task bar that runs along the top of the project window can hold several tools and components. This task bar is also customizable.

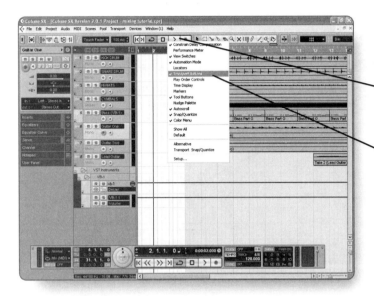

To demonstrate this, let's remove the transport buttons from the task bar.

1. **Right-click** on the **task bar**. The task bar's Component menu will appear.

2. **Click** on **Transport Buttons**. The buttons will be removed from the task bar.

Next we'll restore the transport buttons.

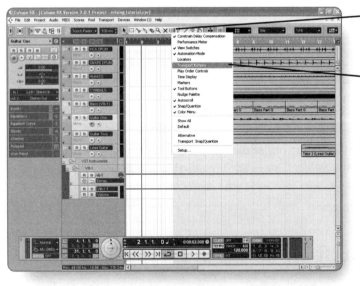

3. **Right-click** on the **task bar**. The Component menu will appear.

4. **Click** on **Transport Buttons**. The transport buttons will reappear on the task bar.

Program Startup Options

By default, when launched, SX will only open the application. If you want to start a new project, you must select New from the File menu. If you want to open an existing project, you'll do so by selecting Open from the File menu. Luckily, SX also provides a way to customize what happens when the application opens.

To change the startup option, we'll first need to open SX's Preferences.

For Windows XP users:

1. **Click** on the **File menu**. The File menu will appear.

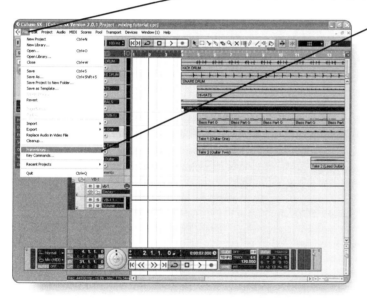

2. **Click** on **Preferences**. The Preferences window will appear.

For Macintosh OS X users:

1. **Click** on the **Cubase SX menu**. The SX menu will appear.

2. **Click** on **Preferences**. The Preferences window will appear.

Next, let's look at how to set the startup options.

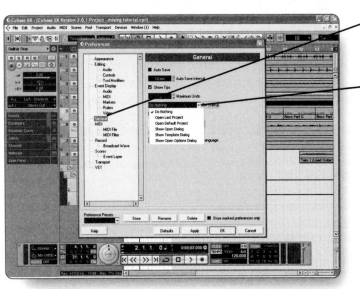

1. Click on **General**. The General Preferences window will appear.

2. Click on the **On Startup menu**. A drop-down menu will appear.

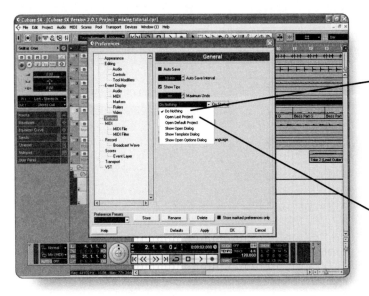

The menu has several options. You should choose the one that suits your workflow preferences.

- **Do Nothing**. This is the default option. When SX launches, no projects will open. From this point, you will have to either start a new project or open an existing one.

- **Open Last Project**. This option automatically opens the last project you were working on. This is helpful if you are spending a lot of time on one particular project.

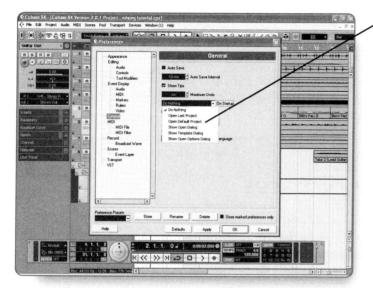

- **Open Default Project**. This option automatically opens the project titled default.cpr. This is useful if you want to create a custom template that will open every time you launch the program.

CAUTION

Creating default.cpr

If you use the Open Default Project option, you will need to have a project titled default.cpr in the SX or SL folder (in the SX or SL package for Macintosh OS X users). This project is not installed during the program's installation; you will need to manually create it.

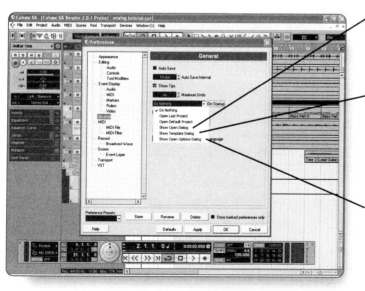

- **Show Open Dialog**. This option automatically displays the Open Project window after starting SX.

- **Show Template Dialog**. This option opens the Template menu when the program starts; it's the same menu that appears when you select New from the File menu.

- **Open Options Dialog**. This option opens a dialog window that allows you to choose either to open a project or create a new one.

> **NOTE**
>
> **Using Cancel**
>
> Selecting Cancel on the Open Options dialog will force SX to open the program itself, just as the Do Nothing option would do.

Workspaces

When we're hungry we go to the kitchen; when we want to relax we go to the den; to brush our teeth we go to the bathroom; and when it's time for sleep we head to the bedroom. Our lives would be a lot more difficult if we only had one room where we had to do everything. The same concept can be applied to workspaces in Cubase SX. A workspace is simply the area that you see on the screen when working in the program; it includes the position and size of all the open windows and toolbars. New to Cubase SX is the ability to create multiple workspaces, each to be used for a different task. For example, you can create a workspace specifically for audio editing, one for mixing, one for MIDI, etc. Once you have a workspace created, you can easily toggle between different workspaces.

Creating Workspaces

Creating a custom workspace is simply a matter of naming the workspace and then opening and positioning the desired windows.

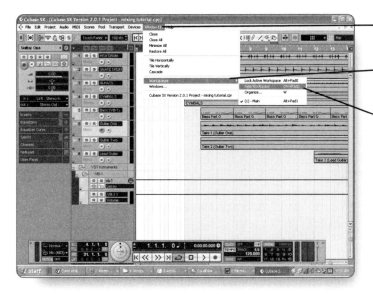

1. Click on **Windows**. The Windows menu will appear.

2. Click on **Workspaces**. A submenu will appear.

3. Click on **New Workspace**. A dialog box will open prompting you to name your workspace.

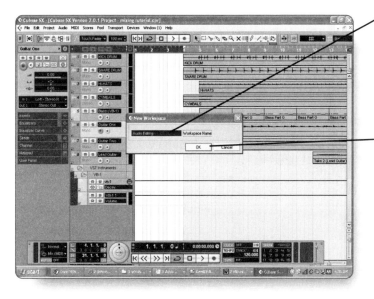

4. Type a **name** for your workspace. It's a good idea to give the workspace a descriptive name. For example, a workspace dedicated to Mixing could be called—Mixing!

5. Click on **OK**. The workspace will be created.

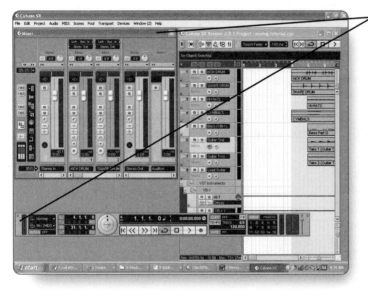

6. Open and **reposition** any windows or toolbars that you would like to be a part of this workspace. The position of the windows and toolbars will be saved with this workspace.

Accessing Workspaces

Once you have several workspaces selected, toggling through them is simply a matter of selecting the desired workspace from the Windows menu.

1. Click on **Windows**. The Windows menu will appear.

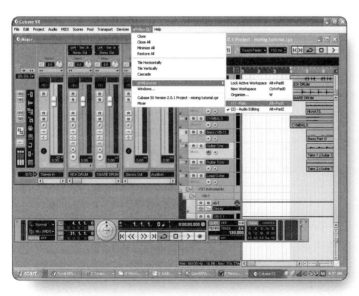

2. Click on **Workspaces**. A submenu will appear.

3. Click on the **name** of the desired workspace that you would like to open. It will appear.

TIP

Workspaces Shortcut

You can set up a key command to toggle between workspaces. Consult the Cubase SX documentation for setting up key commands.

14

File Management—
Audio Pool

The Pool is a window that lists all the audio files that have been either recorded or imported into the project. The Pool is where you will manage project audio files. Each audio recording in SX creates a file in the project's Audio folder. If you are working on a project in which you have recorded several takes to one track, you will have created several audio files for each take. These are large files: One minute of CD standard audio, 16-bit/44.1kHz, stereo, will take up 10MB of memory. Many times, after you have finished capturing a satisfactory take, you will be left with a large number of unused audio files that are taking up space on your hard drive. By using the Pool in SX, you can safely remove any unused audio files from the project to help clean up the project's Audio folder. The Pool is also used to import audio files to your project.

In this chapter, you'll learn how to:

- Import audio files into a project
- Insert audio files into a project
- Remove unused audio files

Importing Audio

You have already learned how to record audio to a track; however, this is not the only way to get audio into your project. Perhaps you have a CD of audio files (drum beats, vocals recordings, and so on) that you want to add to your project. To do this, you will need to import the audio files into your project. We are going to look at how to import the audio files by using the Pool.

NOTE

Tutorial File

For this chapter, you will need to download the chapter14_drumloop.wav audio file from **www.courseptr.com/downloads**. If you don't have access to this file, you can use any existing wave file.

---

1. **Create** a new empty **project** (for more on creating an empty project, refer to Chapter 2).

2. **Set** the **project settings** to the following settings: Sample Rate: 44.100kHz and Record Format: 16 bits (refer to Chapter 2 on making project settings).

NOTE

Audio Properties

The properties of the audio file we'll be importing are 44.100kHz and 16 bits; therefore, we want to set the project's setting to be the same.

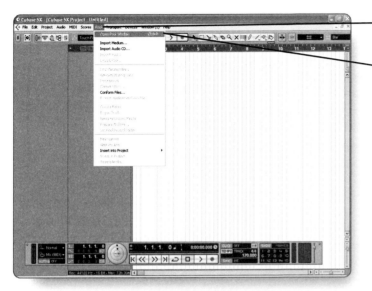

3. **Click** on the **Pool menu**. The Pool menu will appear.

4. **Click** on **Open Pool Window**. The Pool window will appear.

TIP

Pool Window Shortcut

You can also open the Pool window by pressing Ctrl + P (Command + P for Macintosh users).

---

5. **Click** on the **Import button**. The Import Media window will appear.

6. **Navigate** to the **location** on your hard disk where you stored the downloaded audio file.

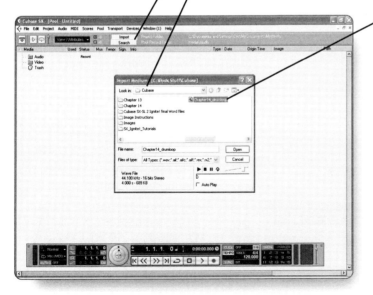

7. **Click** on the **Chapter14_drumloop.wav** file. The file will become highlighted.

NOTE

File Properties

When the file is selected, its properties are displayed on the bottom half of the Import Media window; this helps you ensure that the file's properties match those of your project. You can also preview the file by using the small transport controls in the bottom-right side of the Import Media window.

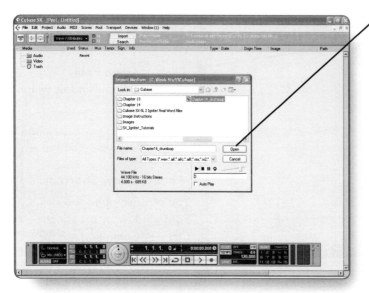

8. **Click** on **Open**. The Import Options window will appear.

The Import Options window is important when importing an audio file. Here you will create a new copy of the file in the project's Audio folder and, if need be, convert the file to match the settings of the project you are importing the file to.

9. **Check** the **Copy File to Working Directory checkbox**.

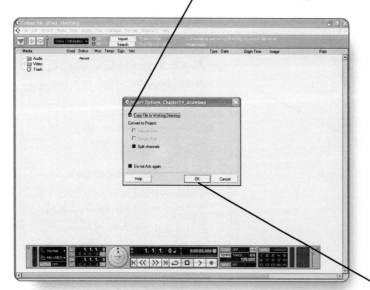

NOTE

Sample Rate and Bit Rate

If you import a file that has a different sample rate or bit rate than the Convert to Project options, Convert Rate and Convert Size will become active. Check these two options to convert the file to match your project.

10. **Click** on **OK**. The file will appear in the Pool under the Audio tree.

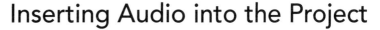

Inserting Audio into the Project

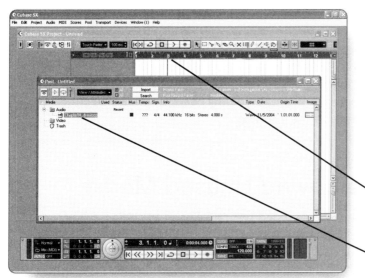

Now that you have the file imported into the project's Pool (and the project's Audio folder), let's add the file to a track.

We are going to import this file so that it starts at bar 3. You may need to restore the Pool window in order to see the ruler in the following steps.

1. **Click** on the **ruler** at bar 3. The project cursor will move to bar 3.

2. **Click** on the **Chapter14_drumloop audio file**. The file will become highlighted.

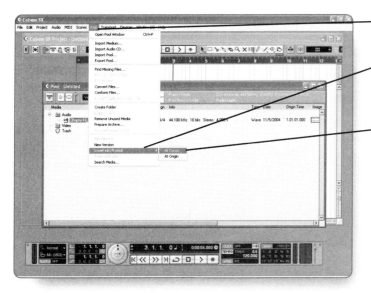

3. **Click** on the **Pool menu**. The Pool menu will appear.

4. **Click** on **Insert into Project**. The Insert into Project submenu will appear.

5. **Click** on **At Cursor**. The audio file will be inserted into a new track and will be set to start at bar 3.

CAUTION

Inserting Tracks

In this exercise we are inserting an audio file into a project that has no audio track; therefore an audio track will be automatically created for the audio file. If you are importing a file into a project that already has one or more audio tracks, you will need to select the correct track before inserting.

Removing Unused Media

If you have recorded several takes to an audio track before getting a satisfactory take, the Pool will be full of audio files that are not being used; however, simply selecting the files in the Pool and deleting them is not wise, because the project will still try to load the files every time you open the project. In addition, you have to be sure that the file you are deleting is in fact no longer being used in the project. We can tell the Pool to automatically remove the files that are no longer being used. This is safer than doing it manually, because the Pool knows which files can be safely removed.

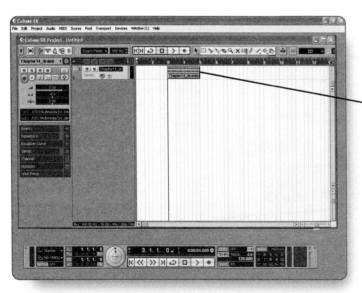

To demonstrate, we are going to remove the drum file that we just finished importing into the project.

1. Click on the **drum loop** that we just inserted into the project. The event will become highlighted.

2. Press the **Delete key** on your keyboard. The event will be removed from the project window.

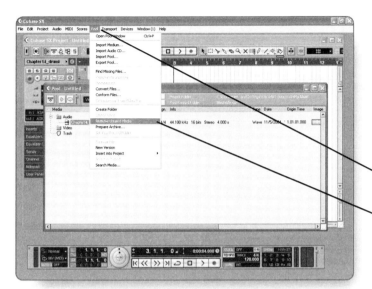

NOTE

Removing Events

Removing an audio event will not remove the file from the Pool.

3. **Click** on the **Pool menu**. The Pool menu will appear.

4. **Click** on **Remove Unused Media**. A dialog window will appear.

NOTE

Pool Window

The Pool window must be in front of any other open windows before you can select any of the functions in the Pool menu.

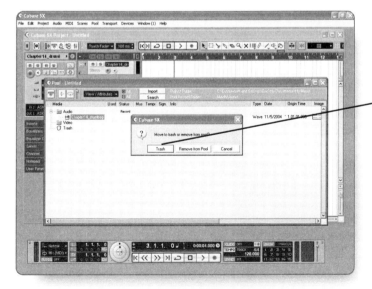

5. **Click** on **Trash**. The file will be moved into the Pool's trash bin.

NOTE

Remove from Pool

Clicking on "Remove from Pool" in step 5 only removes the file from the Pool; it will remain on your hard disk.

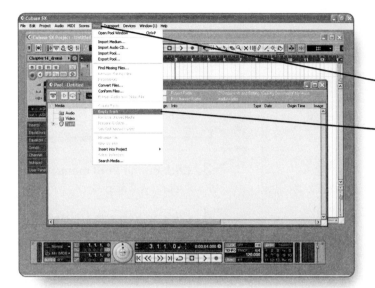

Now let's delete the file from your hard disk (from the project's Audio folder).

6. Click on the **Pool menu**. The Pool menu will appear.

7. Click on **Empty Trash**. The Empty Trash dialog will appear.

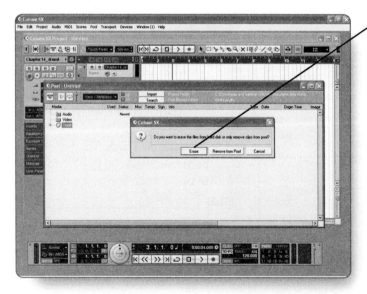

8. Click on **Erase**. The file will now be removed from the Pool's trash bin as well as from the project's Audio folder.

15

Working with Hitpoints

In a few of the previous exercises in this book, we looked at changing the tempo of your project using a fixed tempo setting or even using the tempo track to create tempo changes throughout the project. In these exercises, I mentioned that changing the tempo on a project that already included audio (either by recording or importing) would cause these audio tracks to lose sync with the project's tempo (MIDI tracks are not affected by this). However, SX does offer a feature that will allow you to change the project's tempo without having to worry about the audio drifting out of sync; to do this, you'll use hitpoints. Hitpoints analyze and detect where the beats occur in the audio, and with these points you can then chop the audio into smaller slices. Each slice is lined up to start at the proper timing position (1/4 note, 1/8 note, and so on). It doesn't matter if the tempo changes, your audio will still fit the tempo. We'll also look at how you can use these hitpoints to "tighten up" the timing of an audio recording.

In this chapter, you'll learn how to:

- Create hitpoints
- Slice audio at the hitpoints
- Alter the tempo without affecting audio sync
- Quantize audio

Creating Hitpoints

Before we can dive into slicing and quantizing any audio, you'll first need to create the hitpoints that will determine the locations of the audio slicing. Hitpoints work by analyzing the audio for transients in the recording. A *transient* is the initial sound that is produced when the instrument is played. These transients are used to map the beats and tempo of the audio.

NOTE

Tutorial

For this chapter, you will need to download and open the Hitpoints tutorial project from **www.courseptr.com/downloads**.

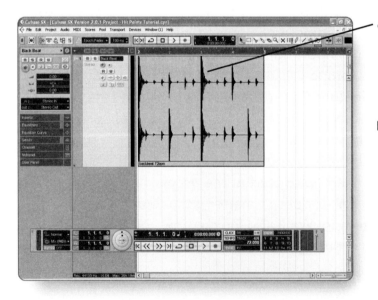

• Looking at the Waveform view of our drum tracks, you can see the transients. The transients are where the drummer first strikes the drum.

Let's now create the hitpoints.

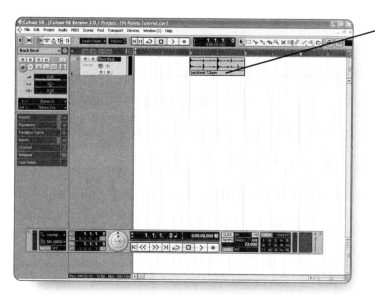

1. Double-click on the **drum audio event**. The Sample Editor window will open.

2. Click on the **Audio menu**. The Audio menu will appear.

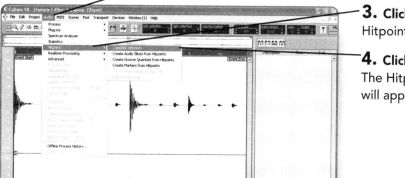

3. Click on **Hitpoints**. The Hitpoints submenu will appear.

4. Click on **Calculate Hitpoints**. The Hitpoint detection settings will appear.

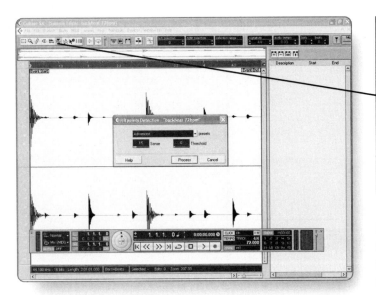

TIP

Hitpoint Detection Shortcut

Alternatively, you can click on the Hitpoint Edit button from the sample editor. The Hitpoint detection settings will appear.

Now let's take a look at some of the settings we need to make so that the points are detected accurately.

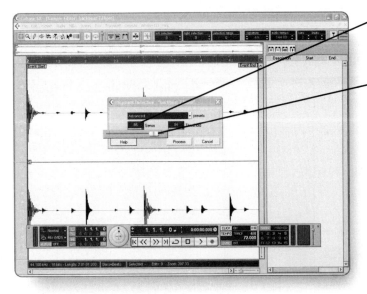

1. Click in the **Sense area**. A slider will appear where you can adjust the sensitivity.

2. Click and drag the **slider**. The higher the sensitivity, the more transients will be detected.

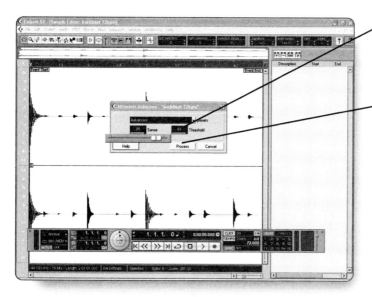

3. **Repeat steps 1 and 2** for the Threshold. The higher the threshold, the less low level transients will be selected.

4. **Click** on **Process**. The Progress indicator window will appear as the detection takes place.

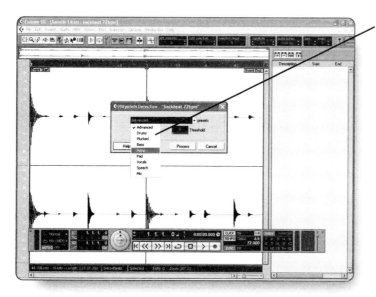

You can also select from a variety of presets for the Sensitivity and Threshold.

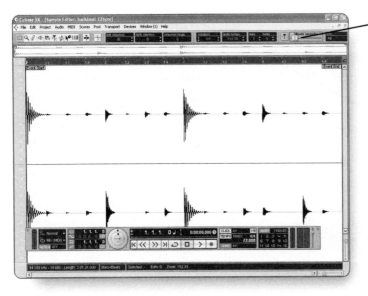

1. Move the **hitpoint sensitivity slider** to the left. The number of hitpoints will decrease. Depending on the resolution of your screen, you may have to close some toolbars or windows to see the hitpoint sensitivity slider.

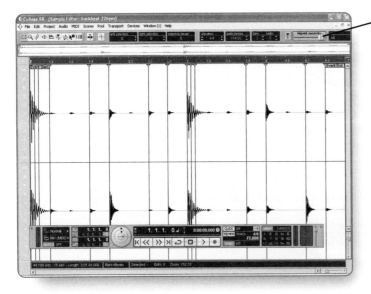

2. Move the **hitpoint sensitivity slider** to the right. The number of hitpoints will increase.

NOTE

Too Many Hitpoints

Perhaps you might be thinking, "the more hitpoints, the better." However, it is possible to have too many hitpoints. Try to set the sensitivity slider so that the main hits are detected. If you have too many hits, there is a risk you can create some unwanted gaps when adjusting the project's tempo.

Slicing Audio at the Hitpoints

Now that you have the points set in the audio file, we are going to take a look at how you can slice up the audio at these points to create smaller pieces of audio. Once the file is sliced up, you can then perform tempo changes to the project without affecting the audio's tempo sync. You can also perform quantization to the audio as we did earlier with MIDI (more on quantization later in this chapter).

To slice the audio:

1. **Click** on the **Audio menu**. The Audio menu will appear.

2. **Click** on **Hitpoints**. The Hitpoints submenu will appear.

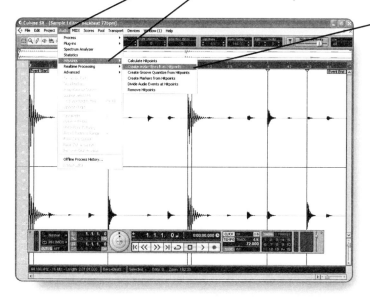

3. **Click** on **Create Audio Slices from Hitpoints**. The sample editor will close, and the audio event in the project window will become an audio part that contains all the slices.

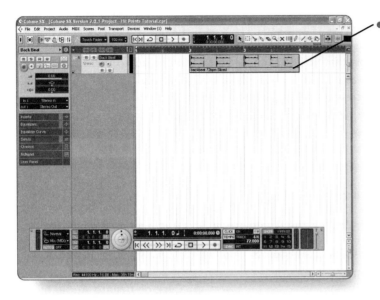

● Once you have sliced the audio event, the event will be replaced by an audio part; this part will contain all the slices.

Changing the Tempo

Now that you have your slices, you can freely change the tempo of your song and not have to worry about the audio being out of sync or time with the project's tempo.

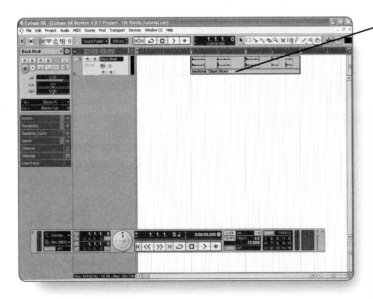

1. Double-click on the **audio part** from the project window. The Audio Part editor will appear.

NOTE

When changing the tempo, it is unnecessary to actually open the Audio Part editor. Here we are opening the editor so you can get a visual representation of what happens to the slices when the tempo is altered.

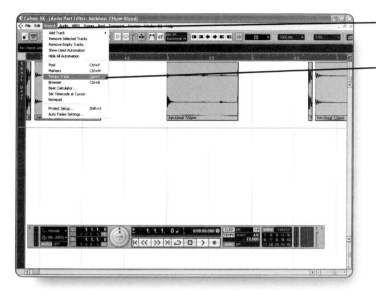

2. Click on the **Project menu**. The Project menu will appear.

3. Click on **Tempo Track**. The tempo track will appear.

4. Double-click on **72** in the Tempo field. The Tempo value will become highlighted.

5. Type in the value **70** and **press Enter**. The tempo will change to 100 BPM.

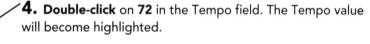

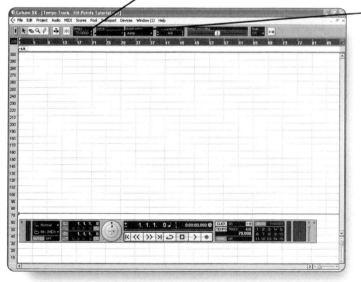

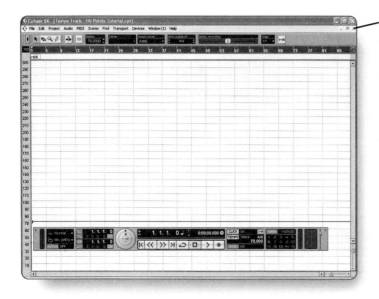

6. Close the **Tempo Track window**.

After lowering the tempo, the slices will now have a greater gap in between them. The slower the tempo is, the larger the gaps will be. This can produce an unwanted chopping effect; let's take a look how we can remove these gaps.

1. Click on the **Edit menu**. The Edit menu will appear.

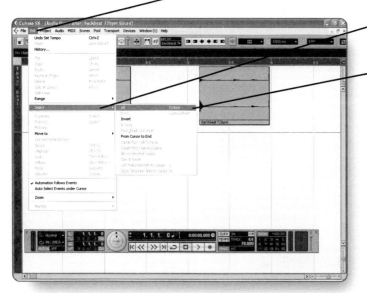

2. Click on **Select**. The Select submenu will appear.

3. Click on **All**. All the slices in the Audio Part editor will become selected.

NOTE

Select All Shortcut

Reminder: You can also press Ctrl + A (Windows) or Command + A (Macintosh) to select all the parts on the Audio Part editor.

4. **Click** on the **Audio menu**. The Audio menu will appear.

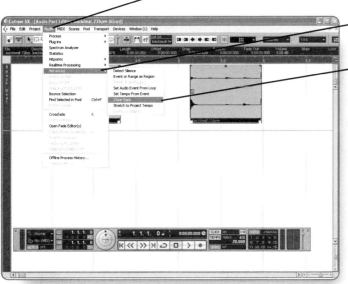

5. **Click** on **Advanced**. The Advanced submenu will appear.

6. **Click** on **Close Gaps**. The Time Stretch progress meter will appear.

NOTE

Close Gaps

Close Gaps works by stretching the audio slice size to cover the gap size. If the gaps are very large, then time stretching may produce some unwanted effects; again, this is if the gaps are very large. In this exercise, the gaps are small enough that you will not hear the effects of the time stretch other than the gaps being closed.

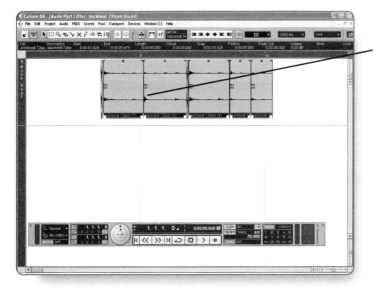

In this figure you can see how the gaps were closed by the Close Gap function.

TIP

Close Gaps with Tempo Change

I recommend closing the gaps after each tempo change, regardless if you are increasing or decreasing the tempo. Although increasing the tempo will not create any gaps between the slices, the function will help take care of any slices that may overlap after a tempo increase.

Quantizing Audio

In Chapter 7 we looked at quantizing MIDI to fix up performances with sloppy timing. This same function can also be applied to audio once you have sliced an audio event.

To quantize audio:

1. Click on the **Edit menu**. The Edit menu will appear.

2. Click on **Select**. The Select submenu will appear.

3. Click on **All**. All the slices in the Audio Part editor will become selected.

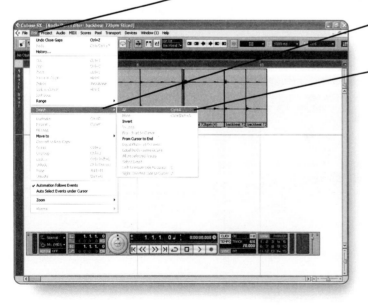

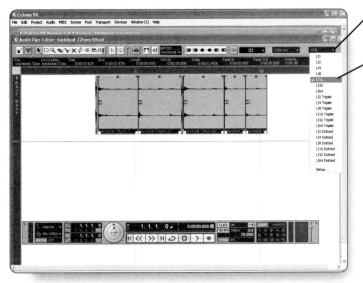

4. Click on the **Quantize menu**. The Quantize menu will appear.

5. Click on **1/16**. The quantize value will now be set to 16th note.

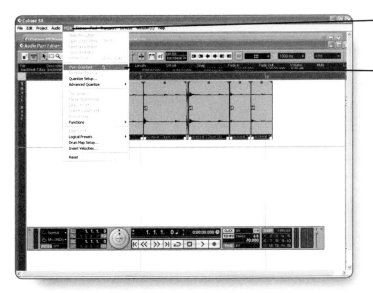

6. Click on the **MIDI menu**. The MIDI menu will appear.

7. Click on **Over Quantize**. The slices in the audio part will be quantized to every 16th note.

NOTE

In the exercise, the result of quantizing this drum loop to every 16th will produce a choppy sounding loop. This is, however, to demonstrate how quantizing can be applied in general. You are encouraged to experiment with quantizing audio.

16

VST Connections and the MIDI Manager

VST Connections is how the program interacts with your audio interface. In SX 2, the engine was redesigned to include some new and improved audio routing methods, and in many ways these new methods work even more like the large mixing consoles in commercial studios. Some of these features include unlimited busses, as well as being able to assign these busses to their own dedicated output on your audio interface (depending on your audio hardware). New to Cubase 3 is another method for controlling your MIDI devices: the MIDI Manager. It allows you to create your own controls for the MIDI devices installed on your computer. You can then use those controls during playback or editing.

In this chapter, you'll learn how to:

- Assign your audio interface's input and output to SX's input and output busses

- Create and remove busses

- Create a MIDI graphical interface

Assigning Your Audio Interface's Input and Output

Up to this point we have been working with the default input and output stereo busses, and for most basic recording and mixing sessions, these busses will be sufficient. However if your PC or Macintosh is equipped with a multichannel audio interface, you may want to change the physical outputs on your card to determine where these default busses are routed to. Let's take a look at how we change the bus assignments.

1. **Click** on the **Devices menu**. The Devices menu will appear.

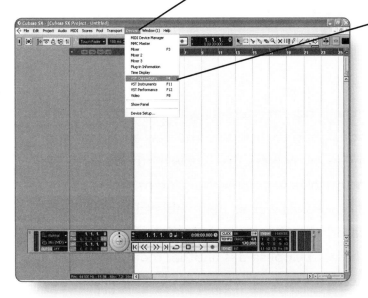

2. **Click** on **VST Connections**. The VST Connections window will appear.

TIP

VST Shortcut

You can open the VST Connections window by pressing F4 (Windows and Macintosh).

Let's begin by changing the physical input that the stereo input bus is connected to.

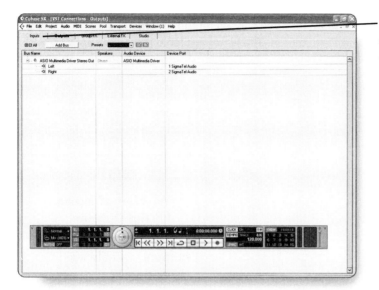

3. Click on the **Inputs tab** at the top of the VST Connections window. The Inputs page will appear.

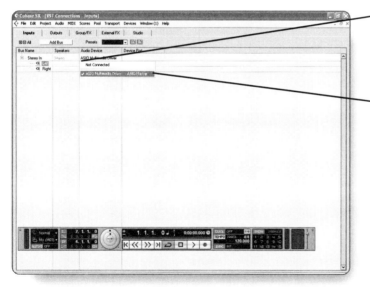

4. Click on the **device** listed on the "Left" row under the ASIO Device Port column. The list of available inputs will appear.

5. Select the **input** that you want to assign to the left channel of the stereo input bus. The input will be reassigned.

> ### NOTE
> #### Channels
> A stereo bus actually consists of two inputs, the left channel and the right channel.

Now assign the input for the right channel of the stereo input bus.

6. Click on the **device** listed on the "Right" row under the ASIO Device Port column. The list of available inputs will appear.

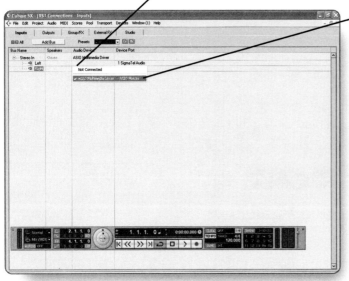

7. Select the **input** you want to be assigned to the right channel of the stereo bus. The input will be reassigned.

NOTE

Number of Inputs and Outputs

The number of inputs and outputs available will depend solely on how many channels your audio interface supports. Check your audio interface's documentation on multichannel operation.

Next let's reassign the stereo output channels.

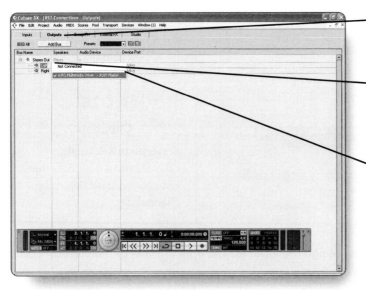

1. Click on the **Outputs tab**. The VST Connection's output page will appear.

2. Click on the **device** on the "Left" row under the ASIO Device Port. The list of available outputs will appear.

3. Select the desired **output** for the left channel. The channel will be reassigned to the new port on your audio interface.

4. **Click** on the **device** on the "Right" row under the ASIO Device Port. The list of available outputs will appear.

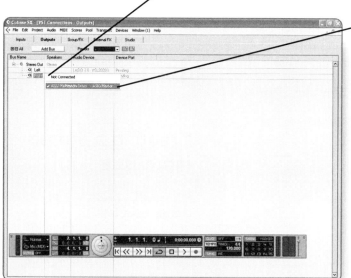

5. **Click** on the desired **output** to which you want right channel to be assigned. The right channel will be reassigned to the new port on your audio interface.

CAUTION

One Input or Output Only

It is not possible for more than one input or output to be assigned to the same output on your audio interface. If you try to assign an input or output to a port that is already being used, that port automatically will be reassigned to an available port.

NOTE

Left and Right Designations

By default, SX will assign the left and right channels of the input and output busses to the first two input and output ports of your audio interface.

Creating and Removing Busses

Like everything else in SX, you have the freedom to make and customize your own busses. You can create multiple input and output busses, either stereo or mono, and for SX users you can also create busses specifically for surround sound work. Let's take a look at how to create your own busses.

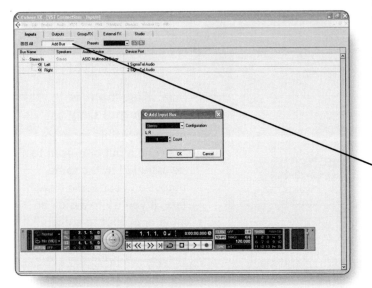

Creating a Stereo Input Bus

We'll start by creating another stereo input bus.

1. Click on the **Add Bus button**. The Add Bus window will appear.

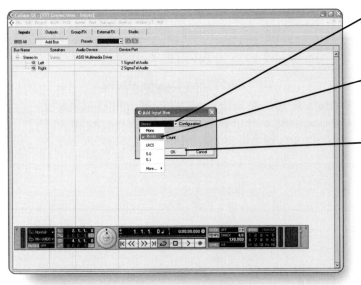

2. Click on the **Configuration menu**. The Configuration menu will appear.

3. Click on **Stereo**. The bus configuration will be set to stereo.

4. Click on **OK**. A new stereo bus labeled Stereo In 2 will be created.

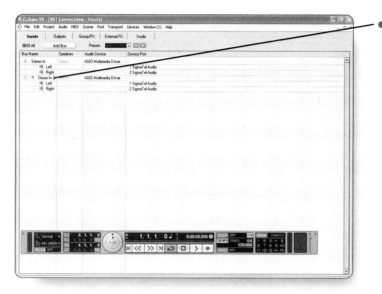

• The new stereo input bus appears in the VST Connection's input page.

Creating a Mono Input Bus

Next we are going to add a mono input bus.

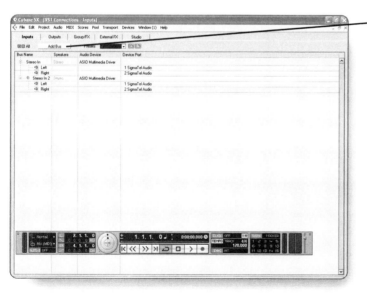

1. Click on the **Add Bus button**. The Add Bus window will appear.

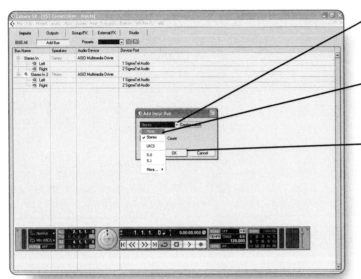

2. **Click** on **Configuration**. The Configuration menu will appear.

3. **Click** on **Mono**. The configuration will be set to create a new mono bus.

4. **Click** on **OK**. A new mono input bus will appear on the VST Connection window labeled "Mono In".

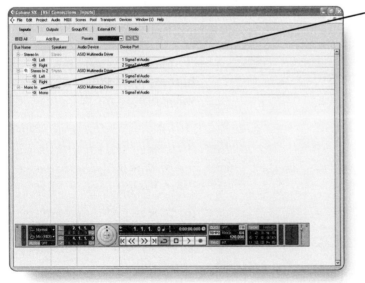

● The new mono input channel created on the VST Connection's input page.

Creating a Stereo Output Bus

Now we are going to look at adding a stereo output bus.

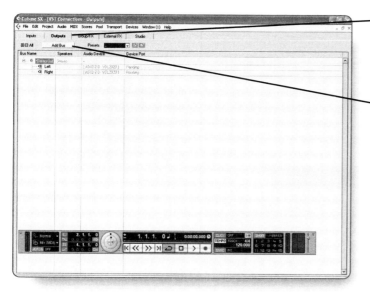

1. Click on the **Outputs tab** at the top of the VST Connections window. The outputs page will appear.

2. Click on the **Add Bus button**. The Add Bus window will appear.

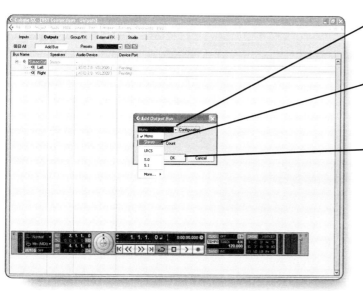

3. Click on **Configuration**. The Configuration menu will appear.

4. Click on **Stereo**. The Add Bus window will be set to add a stereo bus.

5. Click on **OK**. A new output bus labeled Stereo Out 2 will appear in the VST Connection's output page.

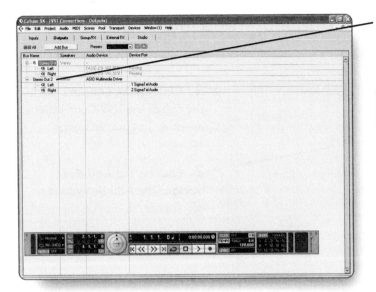

• The new stereo output bus is created on the VST Connection's window.

NOTE

Mono Output Bus

It is possible to create a mono output bus as well. To create a mono output bus, simply select "Mono" in step 4 of the preceding exercise.

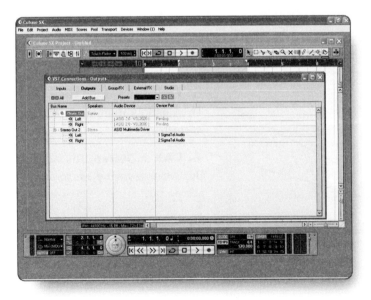

Now we are going to take a look at the Mixer to see how it reflects the changes we made to the input and output busses.

1. **Close** the **VST Connections window**.

2. **Click** on the **Mixer button**. The Mixer will appear.

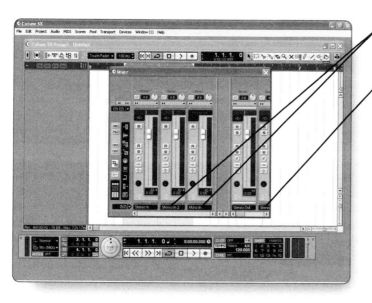

• Here you can see the stereo and mono input busses that were created.

• Here you can see the additional stereo output bus.

MIDI Device Manager

New to Cubase 3 is the MIDI Device Manager. It gives you the ability to access and control your external MIDI devices by building your own graphical interfaces. You can select which elements you would like to create and then, simply by clicking and dragging, you can customize your own interface.

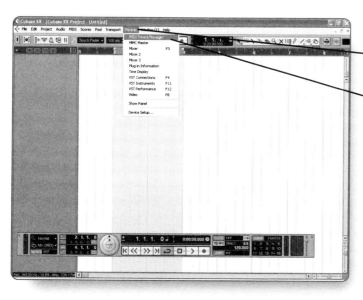

1. Click on **Devices**. The Devices menu will appear.

2. Click on **MIDI Device Manager**. The MIDI Devices dialog box will open.

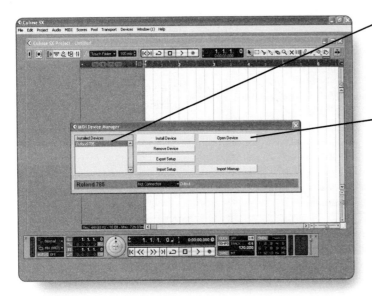

3. Click on your **MIDI device** from the list of installed devices. If your device is not there, you can add it by clicking on the Install Device button.

4. Click on the **Open Device button**. A window will appear where you can configure the display for your device.

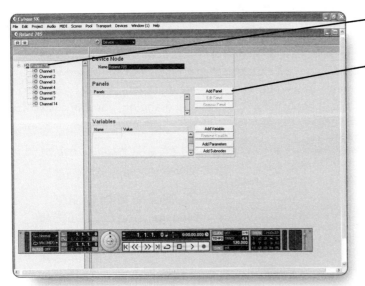

5. Click on the **name** of your device. It will be highlighted.

6. Click on **Add Panel**. You can now add a graphical panel to control your MIDI device.

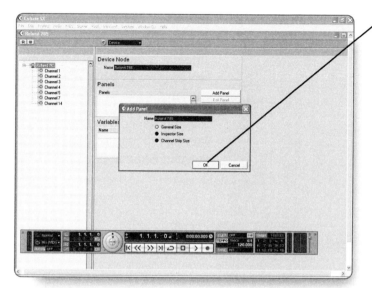

7. Click on **OK** to close the dialog and begin adding components to your panel. Alternatively, you can rename the panel you are creating by typing a new name for it in this dialog box.

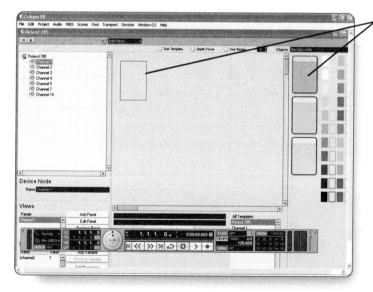

8. Click and drag any **background** to your panel. When you release the mouse button, that background will appear on your panel.

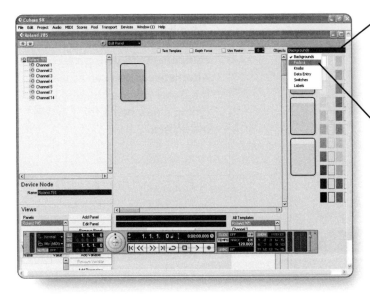

9. Click on the **User Object Categories menu**. A list of different categories of items you can add to your panel will appear.

10. Click on the desired **category**. In this example we selected Faders.

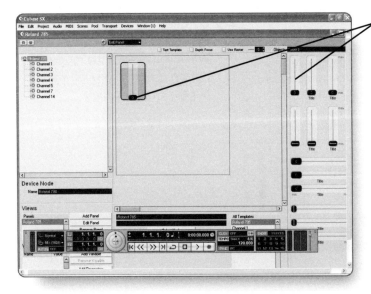

11. Click and drag any **object** from the category you selected onto the panel. When you release the mouse button, the object will appear on the panel. A dialog window may then appear prompting you to configure the element you have just added.

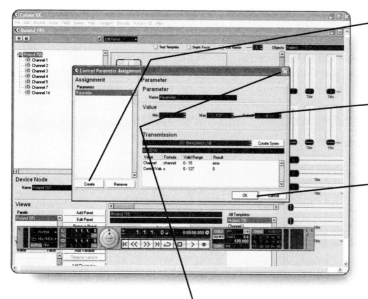

12. Click on **Create**. You will now be able to adjust any of the parameters for the element you have added.

13. Adjust any of the **settings** for the element you have added. You can rename the parameter or change the values.

14. Click on **OK**. The settings you adjusted for this element will take effect.

15. Repeat steps 8–14 to add any other components to your panel.

16. Click on the **x** in the top-right corner to close the window. A dialog box will appear prompting you to save your panel.

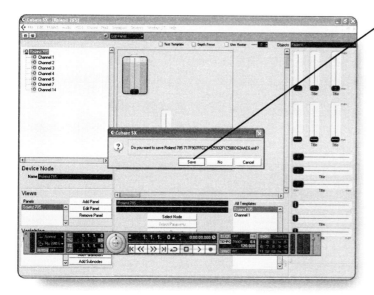

17. Click on **Save**. You will now be able to open and use the panel you created.

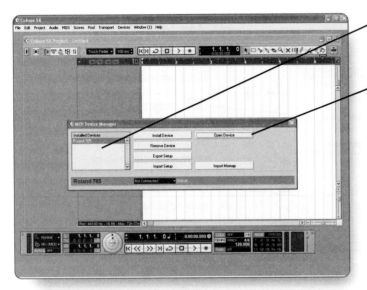

18. Click on the **device** that you would like to open. It will be highlighted.

19. Click on **Open Device**. The graphical interface you created to control your device will open.

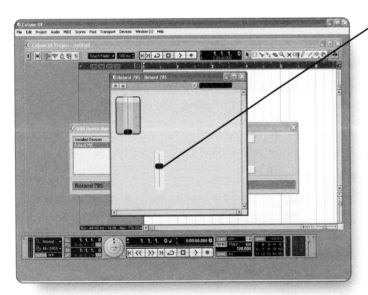

20. Adjust the **settings** of your device using the panel you created.

A
Additional MIDI Editors

In Chapter 7, we looked at editing MIDI with the Key Editor. In this appendix we are going to briefly consider some additional MIDI Editors. Although in most cases the Key Editor will be sufficient for your editing needs, there may be a situation in which you will need a more specific editor; an example would be the Drum Editor, which gives you more control when editing MIDI drum tracks. Or perhaps you would be more comfortable editing with the Score Editor or the List Editor, both of which offer particular strengths.

In this appendix, you'll learn how to:

◉ Convert a MIDI track to a drum track

◉ Edit a drum track in the Drum Editor

◉ Open a MIDI track in the Score Editor

◉ Edit MIDI in the List Editor

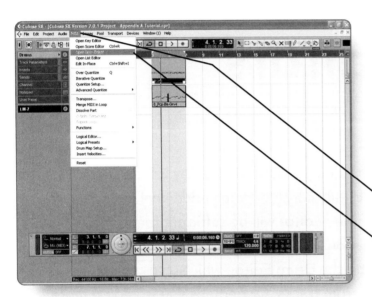

Editing a Drum Track

Now that you have converted
the MIDI track to a drum track,
let's take a look at how to edit
the drum part in the Drum
Editor.

1. Click on **MIDI.** The MIDI
menu will appear.

2. Click on **Open Drum Editor.**
The Drum Editor window will
open.

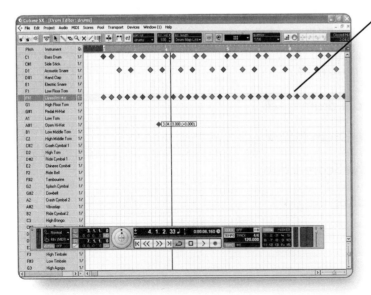

● The first thing you will notice
is that instead of rectangles,
drum notes are indicated by
diamonds. These diamonds
show when the drum will be
triggered (played).

Next we are going to change the
diamond that triggers a closed
hi-hat at one sixteenth beat
before each bar to trigger an
open hat. This will give your
drums more of a swing feel.

> ## NOTE
>
> ### Trigger
>
> In the Drum Editor, I'll be using the term "trigger" instead of "note" to refer to the diamond points. We use the term "note" to describe a pitch reference; however, because drums have no pitch reference, "trigger" is more appropriate.

1. **Click** on the **closed hi-hat note** that is triggered one eighth beat before bar 4. The note will become highlighted.

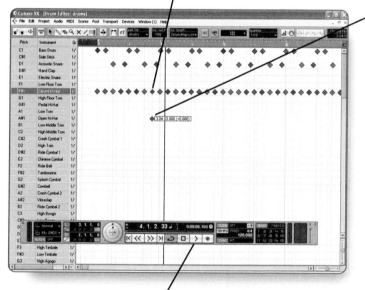

2. **Drag** the **note** down to open hi-hat.

- The Drum Editor will also show by name which piece of the drum kit the notes on your MIDI controller are mapped to. The names shown here are for the general MIDI map. Clicking on the far-left column (to the left of the Pitch column) will audition the drum piece assigned to that pitch.

3. **Repeat step 2** for each trigger that falls one eighth beat before bars 5, 6, and 7.

4. **Click** on the **Play button** to begin playback. An open hi-hat will play one eighth note before each bar, giving your drums more of a swing.

Next, let's manually draw some side stick triggers into our drum part.

1. **Click** on the **drum stick** on the toolbar. The pointer cursor will become a drum stick.

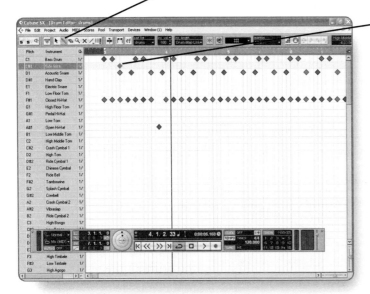

2. **Click** on the **side stick row** on beats 2 and 4 of all bars (3-7). Triggers will be played along with the snare drum on beat 2 and 4 of all four bars.

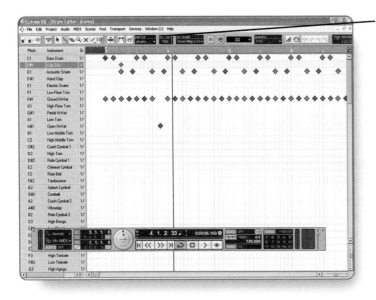

Insert Velocity. When using the Drum Stick tool to manually draw drum triggers, all triggers will set their velocity to the value set here.

TIP

Drum Editor Tools

Most of the tools in Drum Editor work in the same manner as the Key Editor; refer to Chapter 7 for more on these tools.

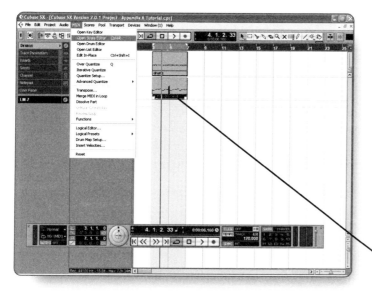

Opening the Score

You may be more comfortable editing your music on a traditional music score. If so, SX comes with a Score Editor that will allow you to do just that.

To demonstrate, we'll open the bass MIDI part into the Score Editor.

1. Click on the **bass part**. The part will become highlighted.

2. Click on the **MIDI menu**. The MIDI menu will appear.

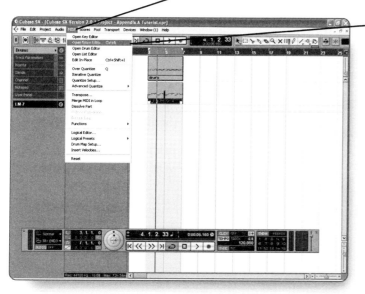

3. Click on **Open Score Editor**. The Score Editor will open with the bass MIDI part in the score.

The Score Editor is a capable, complex editor, and a complete discussion of its features is beyond the scope of this book. For more information on using the Score Editor, consult your SX documentation or *Cubase SX/SL 3 Power!* by Robert Guerin.

NOTE

Score Shortcut

The score may also be opened from Score Menu > Open Selected.

The List Editor

Perhaps the oldest method of editing MIDI data is using a List Editor. A List Editor displays the sequence of notes in a single list. The benefit of the List Editor is that it does not display any spaces that are between notes which, for some, makes it easier to navigate through MIDI parts when editing. In addition, the List Editor displays MIDI information other than note information, such as pitch bends and program changes.

NOTE

MIDI Commands

Commands from your computer tell a MIDI device (synthesizer, drum machine, and so on) which note to play, how hard to play it, and how long to play it. MIDI, however, can be more than just note information. MIDI commands can also tell your synthesizer which sound (patch) to play (program change) and to perform pitch bends. And those are just two examples. There are many different MIDI commands.

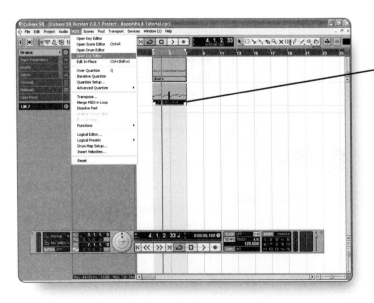

To demonstrate, we'll open the bass part in the List Editor.

1. Click on the **bass part**. The part will become highlighted.

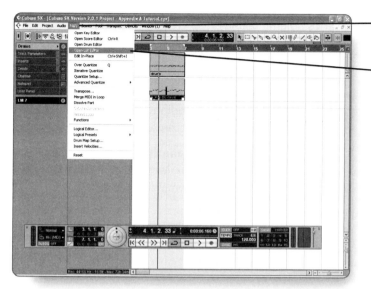

2. Click on the **MIDI menu**. The MIDI menu will appear.

3. Click on **Open List Editor**. The List Editor will appear.

When working in the List Editor, it is possible to type in values for all the MIDI data. This can be helpful when you want to be precise. Let's change the pitch of the second note from a G#0 to a G0.

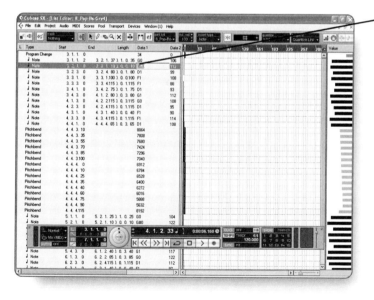

4. Click on the **G#0 note** in the Data 1 column. The note will become highlighted.

5. Type in **G0** and **press Enter**. The note will now be a G0.

In the List Editor, there are several different columns; a brief description of each follows.

• **Type**. This column displays the type of MIDI command.

• **Start**. This column displays the point in the sequence when the command is sent.

• **End**. This column displays the ending point of the MIDI Note commands.

• **Length**. This column displays the length of the MIDI Note command.

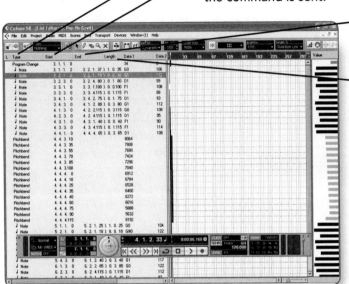

• **Data 1**. This column displays the pitch of the MIDI note.

• **Data 2**. This column displays the velocity of the MIDI note.

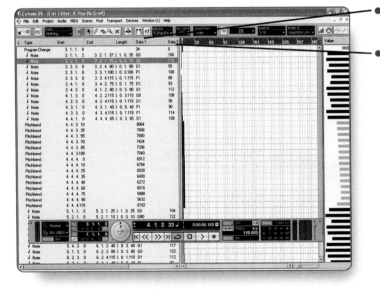

B

Project Tools

In this appendix, we'll consider some of the additional project tools that will give you more control over your SX project and improve your workflow. We'll cover the use of markers, which allow you to quickly navigate through your project or concentrate on certain sections of your project. We'll also work with the tempo track. Earlier we looked at setting your projects to a fixed tempo; with the tempo track we can make tempo changes at any point in the project.

In this appendix, you'll learn how to:

- Create and use markers to help you navigate through your project
- Make tempo changes at various points in a project

Markers and Marker Tracks

Imagine you are working on a project, either by yourself or perhaps with some band mates, and you or your guitar player wants to quickly jump back to the song's intro or to the first verse. In the old days, you would have to stop the playback, rewind the tape to the desired position in the project, and begin playback. This stop and start can slow down your workflow and the creative process. With markers, it's possible to simply click on a button and the project's playback cursor will quickly relocate to the desired position. And since you are working in the computer world, relocation is instantaneous, unlike using a tape machine, which allows you to keep the creative process alive.

Creating Markers

Before you can use markers, you need to create them at the desired points in the project. In the following exercise we are going to create markers that use the basic foundations of a song—verse and chorus.

Let's begin by setting the playback cursor to our first marker position.

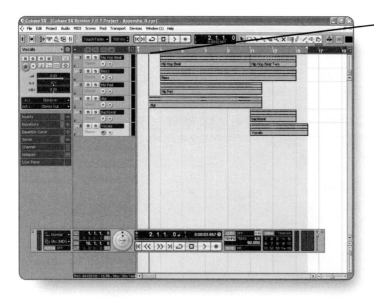

1. **Click** on the **ruler** above the project window at bar 2. The playback cursor will move to bar 2.

Now let's open the Markers window.

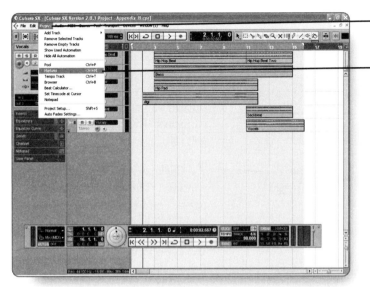

2. Click on the **Project menu**. The Project menu will appear.

3. Click on **Markers**. The Markers window will appear.

NOTE

Markers Shortcut

You can also open the Markers window by pressing Ctrl + M (Windows) or Command + M (Macintosh).

Now let's add a marker and name it "Intro."

4. Click on **Add**. A new marker will appear with the Description column highlighted.

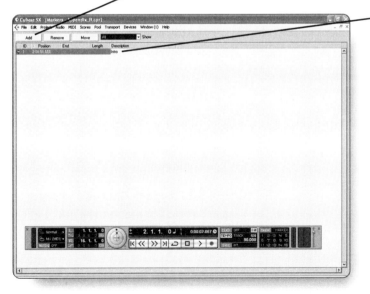

5. Type in **Intro** and **press Enter**. The marker will now be named Intro.

NOTE

Marker Location

Markers are always added at the location of the playback cursor. Before adding a new marker, be sure to place the cursor where you want the marker to be.

Now let's create two more markers, one for the verse and another for the chorus.

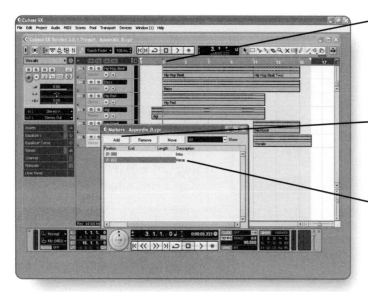

6. Click on the **ruler** at bar 3. You may have to click the restore button so you can see both windows. The playback cursor will relocate to bar 3.

7. Click on **Add** in the Markers window. A new marker will appear and the description will be highlighted.

8. Type in **Verse** and **press Enter**. The marker will now be named Verse.

Now we have two markers. Let's make one more on bar 11.

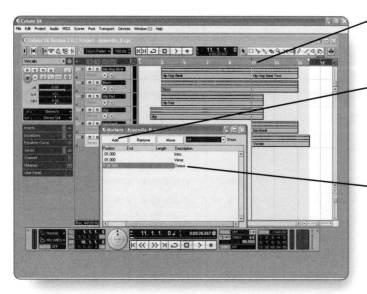

9. Click on the **ruler** at bar 11. The playback cursor will relocate to bar 11.

10. Click on **Add** in the Markers window. Once again a new marker will appear and the Description column will be highlighted.

11. Type in **Chorus** and **press Enter**. The marker will now be named Chorus.

Now that you have markers made for the main parts of the project (Intro, Verse, and Chorus), let's now use them to quickly relocate to their positions.

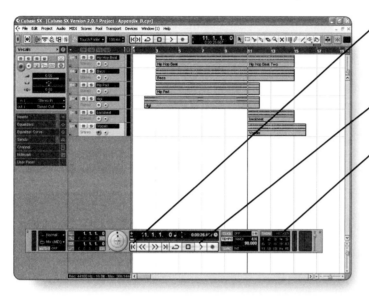

1. **Click** on the **Go to Previous Marker/Zero button**. The playback cursor will relocate to bar 3.

2. **Click** on the **Play button**. The project will begin playback.

3. **Click** on **marker button 3** from the transport panel. The playback cursor will relocate and resume playing from bar 11.

NOTE

Marker Numbering

When adding markers to the Marker window, each new marker is automatically numbered in sequence. The first marker at bar 2 will be marker #1; bar 3 will be marker #2; and bar 11 will be marker #3. Clicking on the marker number from the transport panel automatically will relocate to the position of that marker number. Although there are only 16 marker numbers on the transport panel, you can add more. We'll look at how to access markers higher than 16 next.

Marker Tracks

So now you know how to create and use markers to quickly relocate to predefined positions in the project. Next we are going to learn how you can use marker tracks to get a better visual representation of the markers. Using a marker track will also allow you to access marker numbers higher than 16.

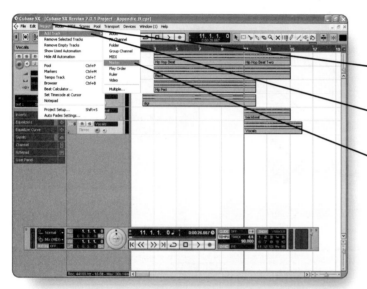

We'll begin by creating a marker track.

1. Click on the **Project menu**. The Project menu will appear.

2. Click on **Add Track**. The Add Track submenu will appear.

3. Click on **Marker**. A Marker Track will appear in the project window.

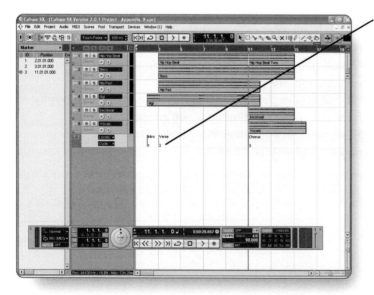

- When the marker track is created you will see the three markers that you created earlier.

Now let's see how to use the marker track to relocate the playback cursor.

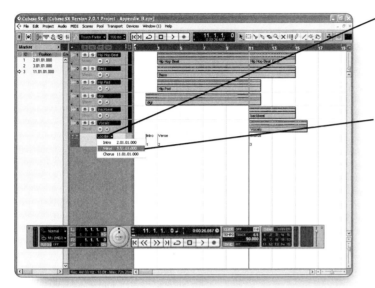

4. Click on the **Locate menu** from the marker track. The Locate menu will appear with the three markers we created earlier listed.

5. Click on **Verse**. The playback cursor will relocate to bar 3.

NOTE

Transport Panel

From the transport panel you can relocate the playback cursor to any of the first 15 marker positions. By using the Locate menu in a marker track, you can relocate to any marker.

The markers we have learned about up to this point are used to mark a time position within the project; they are used mostly to quickly relocate the playback cursor. Next we will look at cycle markers. These are used when you want to not only quickly relocate the playback cursor, but also set both left and right locators around a particular section of the project. Essentially a cycle marker consists of two markers—one to mark the placement of the left locator and one to mark the right locator's position.

Let's create a new cycle marker that will cycle between bars 11 and 15 (chorus) in the tutorial project.

1. Click and drag downward on the track divider until all of the buttons are revealed.

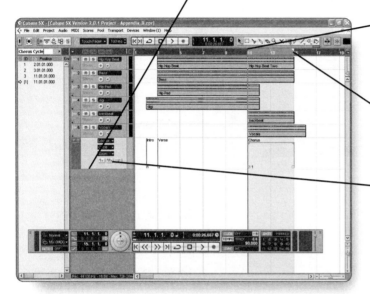

2. Click and drag the **left locator** to bar 11. The left locator will now be located on bar 11.

3. Click and drag the **right locator** to bar 15. The right locator will be positioned on bar 15.

4. Click on the **Add Cycle Marker button** from the marker track.

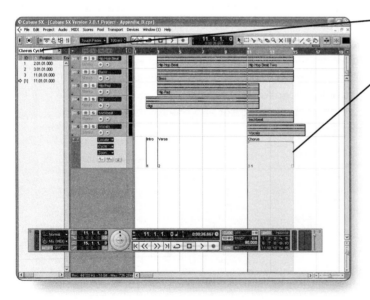

A new cycle marker will appear on the marker track between bars 11 and 15.

- A cycle marker will appear as two separate markers that are joined together by a single line.

Now let's name the cycle marker. Since we created the cycle around bars 11 and 15, which are the chorus, we'll name this marker "Chorus Cycle."

> **NOTE**
>
> **Marker Names**
>
> Although it is possible to name two or more markers with the same name, it is recommended that you vary the names somewhat to avoid confusion. With this exercise we are naming the cycle marker around bars 11 and 15 "Chorus Cycle" so as not to confuse it with the "Chorus" marker we created earlier.

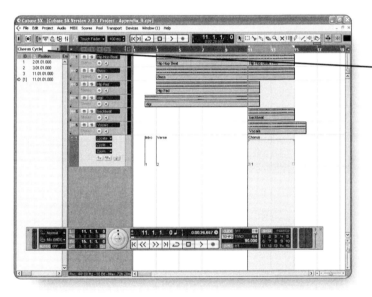

5. **Click** on the **Name field** from the Event Infoline.

6. **Type** in **Chorus Cycle** and **press Enter**. The cycle marker will now be named Chorus Cycle.

Next we are going to relocate the left and right locators so that we can demonstrate using the Cycle menu from the marker track to relocate the left and right locators around the chorus.

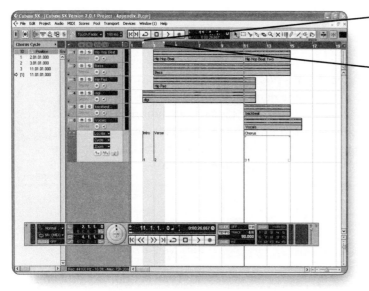

7. **Click and drag** the **left locator** to bar 2.

8. **Click and drag** the **right locator** to bar 4.

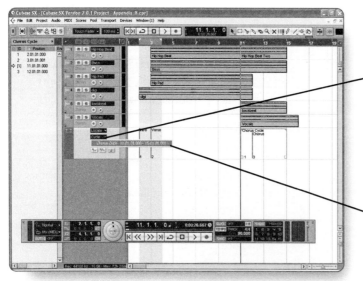

Now let's use the Cycle menu to reset the left and right locators around the chorus.

9. **Click** on the **Cycle menu** from the marker track. The Cycle menu will appear with the list of available cycle markers. Since we created only the one cycle marker (Chorus Cycle), this will be the only available marker.

10. **Click** on **Chorus Cycle**. The left locator will be relocated to bar 11, and the right locator set to bar 15.

One final area of the markers we'll look at is the Zoom to Markers function. This function is available from the markers track. Its job is to zoom into the project vertically so that the contents between cycle markers fill the window.

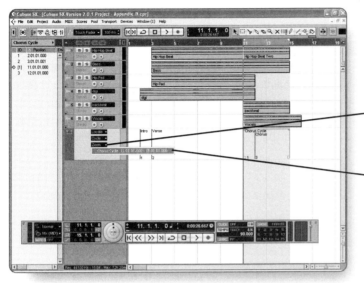

To demonstrate we are going to zoom into the chorus section of our tutorial project. Earlier we created a cycle marker around the chorus.

1. **Click** on the **Zoom menu** from the marker track. The Zoom menu will appear.

2. **Click** on **Chorus Cycle**. The project window automatically will zoom in to the portion of the project set by the cycle marker. You can jump to the next or previous marker by clicking Shift + N or Shift + B, respectively.

Tempo Track

The tempo track's job is to control the tempo of the project over time. In Chapter 3, we learned about setting a fixed tempo, meaning that the project's tempo would remain consistent throughout a song. However, you might have a project in which you want the tempo to increase or slow down. For this you'll use the tempo track.

When working with only MIDI, changing the tempo throughout the project can be accomplished with ease as tempo changes will simply alter how fast the MIDI data is sent to your MIDI devices. However, when you have audio in your project, changing the tempo can be difficult. This is because the audio cannot change how fast it plays to match the tempo changes. Audio has a start point and an end point; the length in between cannot be altered. Therefore it is important that you plan any tempo changes to your project prior to recording audio.

Since the tutorial project for this appendix contains only audio tracks, any changes made to the tempo track after bar 2 (where the audio begins) will cause the audio to be out of sync with the tempo. Therefore, to demonstrate how to use the tempo track, we will alter the project's starting tempo and then make a change back to the original tempo just before the audio starts. This way, after the tempo change takes place, the audio will match the new tempo.

Let's begin by opening the tempo track.

1. Click on the **Project menu**. The Project menu will appear.

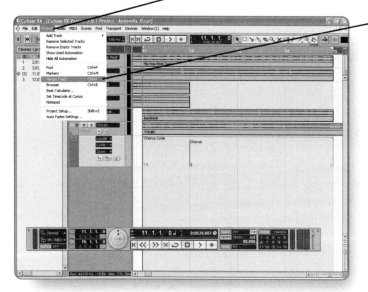

2. Click on **Tempo Track**. The tempo track will appear.

TIP

Tempo Track Shortcut

You can also open the Tempo Track window by pressing Ctrl + T (Windows) or Command + T (Macintosh).

Next we are going to change the tempo to 120 BPM (beats per minute).

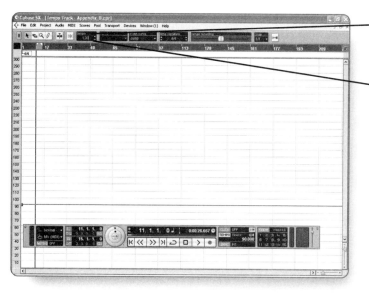

3. **Click** on the **Tempo field**. The Tempo field will become highlighted.

4. **Type** in **120** and **press Enter**. The tempo will now be 120 BPM.

When the audio for this project was recorded, the tempo was 90 BPM; therefore, after changing it to 120 BPM, the audio will no longer line up to the project's tempo. Next we will be making a tempo change, back to 90 BPM, just before the audio begins so the audio tracks will line up to the tempo once again.

5. **Click** on the **Pencil tool**. The pointer will become a pencil.

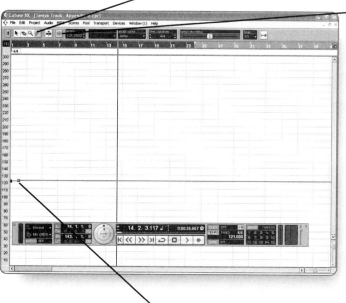

6. **Click** on **Snap**. Snapping will become activated. This is to ensure that the tempo change you draw will snap to the beginning of a bar.

NOTE

Snapping Activation

Depending on your current SX configuration, you might not have Snapping activated. Before continuing to the next step, make sure that Snapping has been activated.

---

7. **Click** on **beat one** of bar 2. A tempo point will be drawn on the tempo track at the start of bar 2.

8. While the tempo point is still highlighted, **click** on the **Tempo field**. The Tempo field will become highlighted.

9. Type in **90** and **press Enter**. The tempo point at the start of bar 2 will lower to 90.

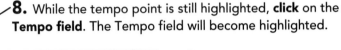
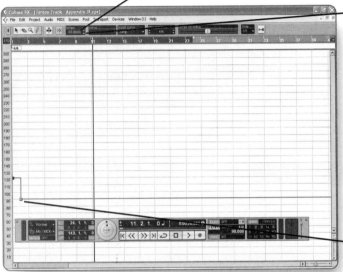

CAUTION

Tempo

When typing the tempo value in step 9, make certain that the tempo point at bar 2 is highlighted.

● After changing the tempo point at bar 2 to 90 BPM you will see the tempo drop on the tempo track.

10. Click on **bar 1** on the ruler above the tempo track. The playback cursor will relocate to bar 1.

11. Click on the **Play button**. Playback will start. Watch the tempo in the transport panel. At first it will read 120 BPM. When the playback cursor reaches bar 2, the tempo will automatically change to 90 BPM.

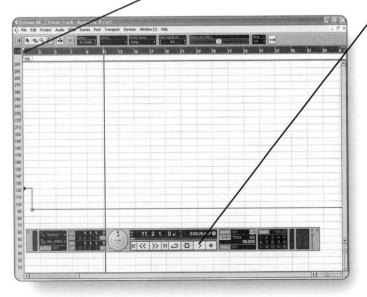

C

The Play Order Track

Typically when you play your project, it plays from left to right in a sequential, linear fashion. New to Cubase SX 3 is the play order track, which allows you to play your sequence out of order. Changing the play order is a two-step project: You start by identifying certain sections of your projects as parts, and then you can rearrange the order of these parts. Once your project has been rearranged, its new order can be made permanent by "flattening" the play order list.

In this appendix, you'll learn how to:

- Create a play order track
- Use the Play Order Editor
- Manage play lists
- Flatten the play order track

Creating the Play Order Track

The play order track is created like any other track in the program.

1. Click on **Project**. The Project menu will appear.

2. Click on **Add Track**. The Add Track submenu will appear.

3. Click on **Play Order**. A play order track will now be created.

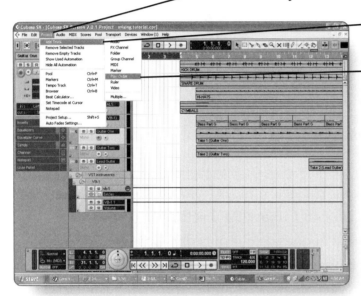

Identifying Project Parts

Once you have a play order track created, you must now label sections of your projects as parts. These parts can later be rearranged in any order.

1. Click on the **Pencil tool**. Your mouse pointer will now look like a little pencil.

2. Click and drag across the **play order track** at the location where you would like to create a part. As you drag, an outline will appear previewing the length of the part.

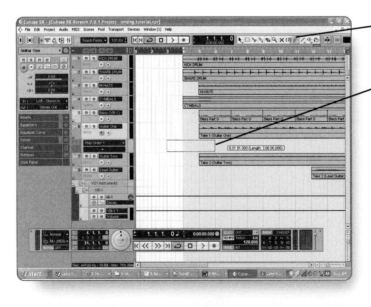

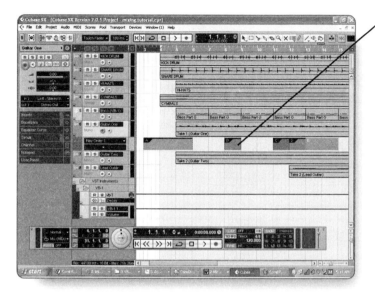

3. Repeat steps 1 and 2 until you have created all the desired parts for your track.

Using the Play Order Editor

The Play Order Editor is a central location for arranging the parts that you have defined. It is comprised of two windows, one that contains all of the parts (the right side) and the other which lists the current play order (the left side).

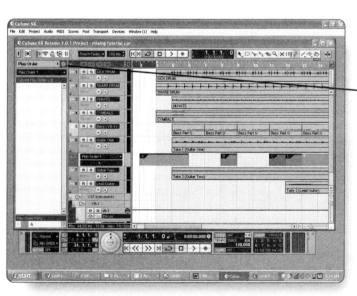

1. Click on the **"e" button**. The Play Order Editor will open and all of the parts you created will appear in the window on the right.

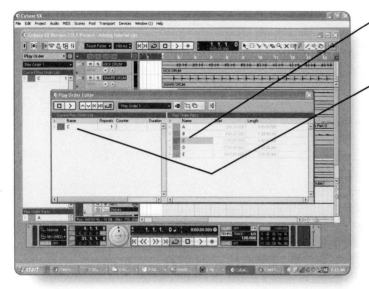

2. **Click and drag** any **piece** from the window on the right to the window on the left.

3. **Release** the **mouse button**. The part will appear in the play order list.

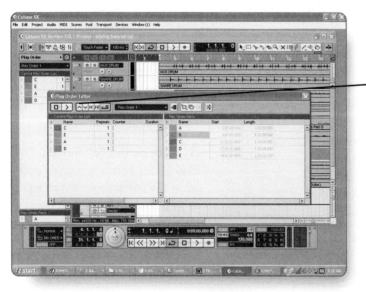

4. **Repeat steps 1 through 3** to add any other parts to your play order list.

5. **Click and drag** any **part** up or down on the list to change its order.

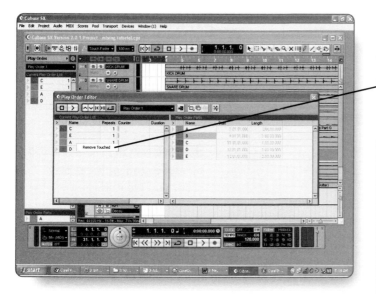

6. **Right-click** (**Ctrl + click** for Mac OS) on any part that you would like to remove.

7. **Click Remove Touched** to remove the part from the list.

TIP

Shortcut for Adding Parts

By double-clicking on any part in the right window of the Play Order Editor, you can add that part to the play order list.

Managing Play Orders

A beneficial feature of the Play Order Editor is that it allows you to create multiple play lists which allows you to experiment with different orders without having to commit to any one. You can also quickly duplicate or remove existing play orders with just a few clicks of the mouse button.

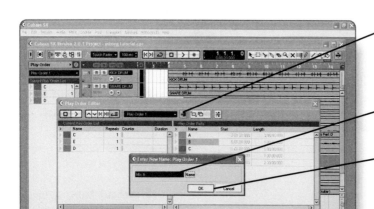

1. **Click** on the **Rename Current Play Order button** to name your play order. A dialog box will appear.

2. **Type** a **name** for your play order in the box provided.

3. **Click** on **OK**. The name will be associated with the play order you created.

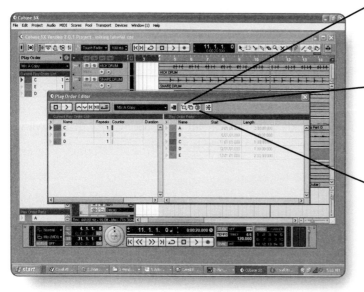

4. **Click** on the **Create New Play Order button** to create a new blank play order. A new play order will be created.

5. **Click** on the **Duplicate Current Play Order button** to create a duplicate of the current play order with all of the existing parts in tact.

6. **Click** on the **Remove Current Play Order button** to remove the current play order. This option is only available if you have created multiple play orders.

Auditioning Play Orders

Once you have your play order parts positioned the way you want them, you can preview how your new sequence will sound. You simply have to select which of your play orders you'd like to audition and then start the playback. You can also jump back and forth through different parts of the order during the playback.

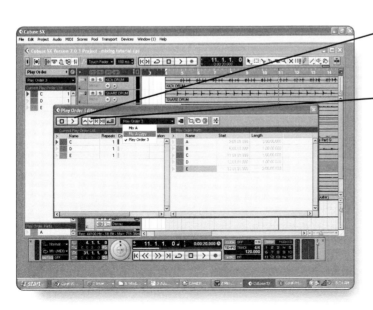

1. Click on the **Activate Play Order Mode button**. This will ensure you are able to play back your play orders.

2. Click the **pop-up menu** to choose from a list of the different play orders that you have created. The list will appear.

3. Click on the desired **play order** that you would like to audition. It will now be loaded.

4. Click on the **Start button**. The playback of your play order list will begin.

5. Click on any of the **Transport Control buttons** to move to different parts of your play order.

Flattening the Play List

Once you have arranged the parts of your track into the desired order, you can flatten them to create a new sequence.

TIP

Back Up Before Flattening

It's a good idea to save your project with a different name before flattening, because flattening will rearrange your sequence to match the play order list. This means that some items and events may get deleted.

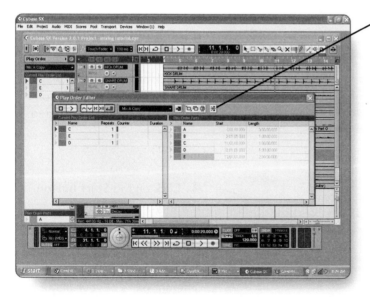

1. Click on the **Flatten Play Order button**. The play order track will be removed, the events in your sequence will be rearranged to match the play order list, and play order mode will be deactivated.

D
Online Resources

The Internet contains vast amounts of information pertaining to Cubase SX. Many sites have dedicated discussions as well as articles with tips and tricks to help you further master the application. In addition to information pertaining to Cubase SX, you can also find loads of sites that offer suggestions and ideas to keep you productive—sites that show you how to get the most from your computers, as well as information about the art of recording and mixing. In this appendix, I will share some of the sites that I have found to be informative and valuable.

Official Steinberg and Cubase SX Sites

www.steinberg.net—The official homepage of Steinberg, makers of Cubase SX. Here you can find more about Steinberg's products and technologies. Steinberg also has an intensive support knowledge base that is helpful if you run into technical difficulties.

www.cubase.net—The official Cubase forums—Get technical support or participate in general discussions to help you get the most out of SX. You can also post in the lounge to get user feedback on your songs.

Sites with Cubase-Related Discussions, Tips, and Tricks

www.espace-cubase.org—A good site with loads of discussions as well as several tips and tricks.

www.cubase.com—Home of the independent and friendly Cubase forum. Offers good discussions as well as a few articles to help you perfect SX.

Plug-in Sites

These sites have loads of information on some of the current third-party effects and VST instruments that can be used in SX.

www.vstcentral.com—Loads of links to many different VST effects! Many of them are free. It's definitely worth checking out.

www.kvr-vst.com—Perhaps the most reputable site with information on several different VST and Direct X effects that can be used in SX.

Computer Maintenance and Tweaking Sites

Use these sites to keep your computer in top shape.

> **www.osxaudio.com**—Perhaps the best source of information on everything to do with keeping your OS X platform purring like a panther.

> **www.musicxp.net**—A great site for all Windows XP users to keep their PCs up to the challenge of audio recording and mixing.

Online Magazines and Other General Audio Sites

These sites offer information regarding computer music and recording in general.

> **eamusic.dartmouth.edu/~book**—A simple straightforward site with loads of articles about the basics of recording.

> **www.stack.nl/~erwint/faq/index.html#two**—Another easy-to-follow website with several articles on audio recording and mixing.

> **www.soundonsound.com**—An excellent magazine. The website has several articles that can be read for free; signing up for a subscription gets you access to the entire site.

> **www.streamworksaudio.com**—Online magazine for recording hobbyists and professionals. Includes several articles regarding music software and discussion forums.

E
Review Questions and Answers

Questions

1. In what window do you configure the project settings?

2. When do you configure an audio track type (stereo or mono)?

3. What function allows you to adjust poor timing on a recorded MIDI performance?

4. What points in the project will be used for punch in and punch out locations?

5. How do you tell SX which tracks you want to record to?

6. Which editor do you use to create Regions from an audio file?

7. What is the safest method of removing audio files from your hard disk that are no longer in use by your project?

8. Which MIDI mode do you use when you want to record a new performance over an existing one?

9. What section of the project window gives you access to all the properties that pertain to a selected track?

10. What key do you hold down while dragging parts and events in order to copy them in the project window?

11. What tool is used to split events or parts?

12. What feature do you use when you want to merge the section where two audio events overlap?

13. When creating Regions, how should you audition so that the selection range is set correctly?

14. What MIDI editor is most commonly used for editing melodic instrument tracks (piano, for example)?

15. What function allows you to remove the load on your computer's CPU created by VST instruments?

16. What feature do you use so that the project's tempo that contains audio can be freely changed?

17. What channel type do you use to combine the output of several audio tracks and VST instruments?

18. What function do you use to control multiple faders by adjusting only one?

19. What are two methods of applying effects?

20. What feature do you use to have any parameter in the Mixer controlled automatically throughout the project?

Answers

1. You configure the project settings in the Project Setup window.

2. You configure an audio track type while you are adding a new audio track to the project.

3. The Quantize function allows you to adjust poor timing on a recorded MIDI performance.

4. The location of the left and right locators will be used for punch in and punch out locations.

5. You tell SX which tracks you want to record to by record arming the desired tracks.

6. You use the Sample Editor to create Regions from an audio file.

7. Using the Remove Unused Media function in the Pool is the safest method of removing audio files from your hard disk that are no longer in use by your project.

8. You use the Overwrite mode when you want to record a new performance over an existing one.

9. The Inspector is the section of the project window that gives you access to all the properties that pertain to a selected track.

10. Alt key (Windows)/Command Key (Macintosh) is the key you hold down while dragging parts and events to copy them in the project window.

11. The Scissors tool is used to split events or parts.

12. You use the Crossfade feature when you want to merge the section where two audio events overlap.

13. When creating Regions, you should audition the selection with the Loop mode active so that the selection range is set correctly.

14. The Key Editor is the MIDI editor most commonly used for editing melodic instrument tracks.

15. You use the Freeze function to remove the load on your computer's CPU created by VST instruments.

16. You use the Hitpoints feature to make sure that the project's tempo that contains audio can be freely changed.

17. You use a group channel to combine the output of several audio tracks and VST instruments.

18. You use the Link Channels function to control multiple faders by adjusting only one.

19. Insert Effects and Send FX (FX channels) are two methods of applying effects.

20. You use automation to have any parameter in the Mixer controlled automatically throughout the project.

Index

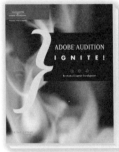